UNTIL HE COMES

REFLECTIONS AND COMMENTARIES ON THE
NEW LITURGICAL READINGS FOR THE
WEEKDAYS OF ADVENT

UNTIL HE COMES

Reflections and Commentaries on the New Liturgical Readings for the Weekdays of Advent

Reflections by
CHARLES E. MILLER, C.M.

Commentaries by
JOHN A. GRINDEL, C.M.

alba house — A DIVISION OF THE SOCIETY OF ST. PAUL
STATEN ISLAND, NEW YORK 10314

Library of Congress Cataloging in Publication Data

Miller, Charles Edward, 1929-
    Until He comes.

    1. Advent--Meditations. I. Grindel, John A.
II. Title.
[BX2170.A4M5]   242'.33   72-8565
ISBN 0-8189-0255-8

Imprimi potest:

   Joseph S. Falanga, C.M.
   Vice Provincial, Los Angeles Vice Province

Nihil obstat:

   Francis D. Pansini, C.M.
   Censor Deputatus

Imprimatur:

   + Timothy Manning
   Archbishop of Los Angeles
   May 18, 1972

The imprimi potest, nihil obstat, and imprimatur are official declarations that a book or pamphlet is free of doctrinal or moral error. No implication is contained therein that those who have granted the imprimi potest, nihil obstat and imprimatur agree with the contents, opinions or statements expressed.

   Copyright 1972 by the Society of St. Paul, 2187 Victory Blvd., Staten Island, N.Y. 10314.

Designed, printed and bound by the Fathers and Brothers of the Society of St. Paul, 2187 Victory Blvd., Staten Island, New York, as part of their communications apostolate.

TABLE OF CONTENTS

Preface vii

PART ONE: The First 3 Weeks of Advent 3

Monday of the First Week 5
Tuesday of the First Week 9
Wednesday of the First Week 12
Thursday of the First Week 15
Friday of the First Week 17
Saturday of the First Week 20
Monday of the Second Week 23
Tuesday of the Second Week 25
Wednesday of the Second Week 28
Thursday of the Second Week 31
Friday of the Second Week 34
Saturday of the Second Week 36
Monday of the Third Week 39
Tuesday of the Third Week 42
Wednesday of the Third Week 45
Thursday of the Third Week 48
Friday of the Third Week 51

PART TWO: December 17th—24th 55

December 17 57
December 18 59
December 19 63
December 20 66
December 21 69
December 22 73
December 23 76
December 24 79

PART THREE: Saints' Days During Advent 83

November 30: Feast of St. Andrew, Apostle 85
December 3: Memorial of St. Francis Xavier 87
December 7: Memorial of St. Ambrose, Bishop 88
December 8: Solemnity of the Immaculate Conception 89
December 13: Memorial of St. Lucy, Martyr 92
December 14: Memorial of St. John of the Cross 93

Index to Biblical Passages 95

PREFACE

THE SEASON OF ADVENT

The season of Advent in Rome began during the sixth century as a joyful liturgical preparation for Christmas, though elsewhere a period of ascetical preparation had been initiated earlier. Eventually the more penitential character of the Gallican Advent in particular spread its influence, and the Roman liturgical Advent took on an ambivalent nature as could be seen in the retention of the "Alleluia," a song of joy, together with the use of violet vestments, a sign of penance.

In the liturgical reform directed by Vatican II, Advent has been restored to a time, not of penance, but of joyful expectation. And quite correctly, for the anticipation of a joyful event should itself be joyful. Though the "Gloria" is not a part of Sunday Masses during Advent, it is omitted not because we are sad or sorrowful, but only so that on Christmas our singing of this great song may in a certain way be a new experience for us.[1] Perhaps unfortunately the violet vestments have been retained, and no official explanation of their continued use has been forthcoming.

Though Advent was instituted to prepare the faithful for the celebration of the birth of Jesus Christ, it soon took on also an eschatological sense. And so our Advent is a twofold preparation: for the birth of Christ and for his coming at the end of time. In the first half of the season, from the beginning of Advent through December 16, the emphasis is on the final coming of Christ; in the second half, from December 17 through December 24, the em-

---

[1] Cf. the restored *Calendarium Romanum*, page 61.

phasis turns to the first coming of Christ in his birth. The prefaces assigned for these divisions reflect the two themes, but it should be remembered that this is a matter of emphasis only, not of exclusiveness. The two themes tend to intermingle in the readings and prayers throughout the entire season.

There seems to be no problem in viewing Advent as a preparation for the second coming of Christ. The second coming is still in the future, and we prepare for something which is yet to come. But there is something of a difficulty in understanding how Advent can be a preparation for an event which has already occurred, and the birth of Jesus belongs to the past. The solution lies in the doctrine of the liturgical "now," the fact that in the liturgy God uses his almighty power to give a current reality to the events of salvation history. Pope St. Leo the Great, who died in 461, reflected the early tradition of the Church when he said in a Christmas sermon: "All the things which Jesus did for us in his humble state belong to the past; nevertheless, today's feast renews for us the blessed coming of Jesus, born of the Virgin Mary."[2] Centuries later another Pope, Pius XII, wrote: "The liturgical year devotedly fostered and accompanied by the Church is not a cold and lifeless representation of the events of the past, or a simple and bare record of a former age. It is rather Christ himself who is ever living in his Church. His mysteries are ever present and active. . . ."[3] The Second Vatican Council confirmed this doctrine:

> *Within the cycle of the year the Church unfolds the whole mystery of Christ, from the incarnation and birth until the ascension, the day of Pentecost, and expectation of blessed hope and of the coming of the Lord. Recalling thus the mystery of redemption, the*

[2] Sixth Christmas Sermon.
[3] *Mediator Dei,* 165.

Church opens to the faithful the riches of the Lord's powers and merits, so that these are in some way made present for all time, and the faithful are enabled to lay hold upon them and become filled with saving grace.[4]

The *Constitution on the Sacred Liturgy* also reminds preachers that the character of the liturgical sermon should be "that of a proclamation of God's wonderful works in the history of salvation, the mystery of Christ, ever made present and active within us, especially in the celebration of the liturgy" (35).

This Christian tradition of the liturgical "now" is a continuation of the Old Testament notion of liturgy. God's saving acts of the past were presented to the people as a present reality so that they could respond to them. This idea is clear particularly from the nature of the material found in the book of Deuteronomy.

Unfortunately some have implicitly rejected the Liturgical "now" because they have been turned away by the explanation offered by some writers of how such a thing can be. Let the theologians and liturgists discuss their theories. We should consider and study their proposals, but explanations are not a part of doctrine. And the doctrine of the Church is that Advent is properly a preparation for the birth of Jesus Christ, as well as for his second coming, because the mystery of his birth is made present and active within us by means of the sacred liturgy.

Advent, then, stands somewhere between the two comings of Christ. Its joyful celebration reflects the meaning of Christian living as it enables us to share in the salvific coming of Christ in history so that his future coming may one day be a reality. The liturgical readings from the Old Testament help us develop a sincere spirit of longing and

---

[4] *Constitution on the Sacred Liturgy*, 102.

expectation, while the gospels gradually unfold the meaning of his incarnation and life among us. With faith in the gift of his saving mysteries we can work with hope toward the day of his final coming as we live our lives of Christian love.

This book contains a short commentary and reflection on each of the lessons and gospels of the weekdays of Advent. The COMMENTARIES have been composed in an objective fashion, without any attempt to relate the readings to each other or to the liturgy of the season. The REFLECTIONS are illustrations of how the scriptural material can be developed into a meditation or brief homily suitable to the meaning of Advent. The authors sincerely hope and pray that God will see fit to make this book a source of inspiration to many and an aid to the Advent preacher, while they recognize that it can never substitute for one's own prayer, study, and creativity. May the hearts of all of us be filled with wonder and praise as we wait in joyful hope until He comes!

UNTIL
HE
COMES

PART ONE

The First 3 Weeks Of Advent

MONDAY OF THE FIRST WEEK

ISAIAH 2:1-5

This passage is not just a description of what the future will bring. Rather, it is primarily an ardent invitation to Israel to walk in the light of the Lord (v. 5), i.e., to accept the Lord as her God and king and to turn away from idols (2:6f) and do His will, showing justice to the poor and needy (Ch. 1). If Israel will do this, then Jerusalem and its Temple will be recognized by all the nations as the place where God has chosen to dwell and they shall stream to Jerusalem to worship God and to hear His word of instruction. From Jerusalem God, ruling in justice, will then arbitrate between the nations and settle their disputes so that peace will reign on the earth with all men laying aside their weapons. But all this will happen only when Israel once again turns to the Lord.

Reflection

Human beings of all times have yearned for peace. Isaiah in the Old Testament prophesied that peace would come from Israel, provided the people learned to walk in the light of the Lord. He said that if Israel would turn to the Lord, the nations would stream to the house of the God of Jacob to seek instruction as to how to walk in the paths of the Lord. What a beautiful picture he painted: "They shall beat their swords into plowshares and their spears into pruning hooks; one nation shall not raise the sword against another nor shall they train for war again."

Isaiah did not understand that his words would be fulfilled only in the Church, the new Israel. With the coming of Christ the angels heralded the message of "peace on earth." But has the Church failed as did Israel? Where is the peace which Jesus came to bring?

In one sense the kingdom of peace and justice is still in the future. It will be realized only in the final coming of

Christ. We, like the Israelites, are a people who must look to the future. On the other hand, we should not expect the final coming of Christ to effect a sudden reversal in the state of the world. We must work for the final coming of Christ by making the Church, that is, ourselves, as much like the final kingdom of justice and peace as possible. Transforming the world through Christ is a gradual process. To draw men to Christ in the Church is the first step. Living as Christ has taught us, with love for all men, can move people to say, "Come, let us climb the Lord's mountain, to the house of God, that he may instruct us in his ways and we may walk in his paths." If the nations are ever to beat their swords into plowshares, we must beat down our own personal feelings of hatred and contempt into love and concern. If the nations are ever to turn their spears into pruning hooks, we must turn our self-seeking into generosity and service. Should we look to the future for a kingdom of peace? Yes, but we must realize that the future comes to be only because of the present.

ISAIAH 4:2-6 *(A Cycle)*

> *Israel has sinned by turning to idols and forgetting the poor and needy (see chapters 2-3). But there will come a day when the Lord shall come and purge Israel of her sins (v. 4). Afterwards the Lord will pour out upon the survivors of the purge abundant blessings which will be a source of honor and glory for them (v. 2). Moreover, the survivors of the purge will be holy, i.e., consecrated to the Lord, and listed among the living in God's census book (v. 3). Such blessings will come upon Jerusalem because the Lord will once again be in their midst as He was with them during their journey through the wilderness (cf. Ex. 13:21 to Is. 4:5) and will protect them from all adversity. God's protection in verse 6 is being painted in terms of the hut which was set up in the vineyard to protect workers from the heat of the day as also from the rain.*

Reflection

The prophet Isaiah foresaw a day when the Lord would come to purify Israel of her sins. It was not really a gloomy prophecy since Isaiah promised that the Lord would thereafter pour out his blessings upon the faithful remnant of his people.

Advent, besides preparing us for Christmas, looks toward the final day of the Lord when he will come again to purify the whole world. Sometimes we think of the end of the world as a time of terrible destruction, a pretty gloomy outlook. Actually we should long for that coming because God will not destroy the world; he will bring it to perfection. God does not destroy what is good, only what is evil. And the world is good, at least basically. The world does need a purification, and we can get a hint from Isaiah of what God's final action will be, for he says that God will wash away the filth of the daughters of Zion, that is, of the people. It is people who bring evil into the world. When all people are purified by God our world will emerge in a new beauty. God's glory will then be a shelter and protection from any further evil.

Despite all of the evil and hatred in our world now, we should never fall into a pessimistic or despairing spirit. Optimism and hope should characterize our outlook. No matter what others may do, our concern should be to work with God in his purifying action by cleansing ourselves of sin here and now. Our prayer should be: "In your mercy keep us free from sin and protect us from all anxiety as we wait in joyful hope for the coming of our Savior, Jesus Christ."

MATTHEW 8:5-11
> *This episode is one of the ten miracles related in chapters 8 and 9 which are meant to show that the messianic era has arrived in Jesus. The point of this*

particular story is that Gentiles will be admitted into the Messianic banquet, i.e., into the kingdom of God, along with the true Israelites (vv. 11-12). *The reason, as seen from the context, will be that these Gentiles will have faith in Jesus contrary to the lack of faith among many of the Jews. The kind of faith that one needs to enter into the kingdom is the unconditional faith of the centurion who has absolute trust in Jesus and in his authority.*

Reflection

The centurion in today's gospel was a man of faith and humility. He had the faith to recognize that Jesus possessed the power to cure his paralyzed servant, and he had the humility to admit that he himself could do nothing to help his servant, that he needed Jesus. At first glance this gospel may strike us as a strange reading for the first weekday of Advent. Actually, however, the faith and humility of this military man serve to remind us of what our attitude should be during this season as we prepare to celebrate Christmas.

Jesus came into our world to cure the human race paralyzed by sin. He wanted to free us of a spiritually crippling disease so that we could live a full, human life as children of God. But he does not force his cure on anyone. First, we must have faith that Jesus, and Jesus alone, has the power to help us. Secondly, we have to be humble enough to admit that we need Jesus, that of ourselves we can do nothing, that all human resources are insufficient to make us spiritually sound. Jesus offers us his healing power in the sacraments, especially in the Eucharist. The effect of the Eucharist upon us is not instantaneous, as was the power of Jesus upon the paralyzed boy, mainly because our faith and humility are not deep enough. To help us grow in faith and humility the Church has adapted the words of the centurion and put them on our lips before we receive the Eucharist: "Lord, I am not worthy to receive you, but only say the word and I shall be healed."

If we make those words an expression of real faith and humility, then our celebration of Christmas will take on more meaning, for Jesus was born to cure human beings paralyzed by sin.

TUESDAY OF THE FIRST WEEK

ISAIAH 11:1-10

> *In chapter 10 Isaiah described in terms of the cutting down of a forest the destruction which Assyria, as God's unknowing instrument, would bring upon Judah for her sins. Now comes a word of hope and promise. Once Judah has been chastized the Lord will raise up a new king from the line of David and will be active within him, bestowing upon him all the qualities of the ideal king. This king will have a perfect knowledge of God's law and how to apply it and his delight will be to worship the Lord and do his will and he will rule with justice. This will be a time of peace, a return to the conditions of paradise, not only for Judah but for the whole world because at that time all men will acknowledge the Lord, do his will, and seek out his representative.*

Reflection

Today's lesson is preceded by a passage which describes Judah, destroyed by invading Assyrians, as a forest cut down and burned. A stump remains among the ruins; it is symbolic of Jesse, the father of David from whom Judean kings were descended. The image of the shoot coming from the stump indicates that the dynasty will not die out. It is a hopeful picture, for the prophet says that "from his roots a bud shall blossom."

Isaiah probably wrote of some ideal Davidic king who would meet the needs of the people through the spirit of God possessed by him in a special way. It is not at all likely that Isaiah had in mind the person of the Messiah as we know him. The Church, however, reading this passage in the light of further revelation understands that Isaiah's prophecy of the ideal king was eminently fulfilled in the person of Jesus Christ, himself of the Davidic line. Jesus was a unique king, one who could call both God and David his father. As the angel said to Mary of her son, "Great will be his dignity and he will be called Son of the Most High; and the Lord God will give him the throne of David his father (Lk. 1:32). Jesus was the end of the Davidic line since he completed it. After him there was no need for another king to succeed him, for "his reign will be without end" (Lk. 1:33).

The prophet Isaiah would have been thrilled into ecstasy had he known that the hope which he held out for his nation was to be realized in Jesus Christ, the God-man. And yet how easy it is for us to take the reality of Jesus Christ for granted. The story of his birth in Bethlehem, David's city, we have heard since we were children. Perhaps we still have only a child's appreciation of its meaning. We should pay heed to the words of today's preface: "When Jesus humbled himself to come among us as a man, he fulfilled the plan God formed long ago and opened for us the way to an eternal kingdom." During Advent we should meditate on this great truth so that we may see how much we need to give thanks and praise to God for sending his son to be our king.

LUKE 10:21-24
The first half of this reading is a prayer of thanksgiving which Jesus is depicted as offering to the Father when the seventy-two disciples return from their first missionary journey. Jesus thanks the Father for having

allowed the disciples to grasp his message about the kingdom of heaven and to experience the power of the kingdom (see 10:17). This has happened because the Father has willed it and caused it to happen. For even though knowledge of the kingdom is revealed through the words and deeds of Jesus, only those can grasp this message and experience the power of the kingdom to whom the Father gives the ability. Then Jesus turns to the disciples and tells them that what they have grasped and experienced is what the kings and prophets of the Old Testament had looked forward to and spoken of.

Reflection

Scholars maintain that William Shakespeare was a great success not only because he possessed literary genius but also because he was born at the right time and in the right place. When he came upon the scene, the English language and the drama had developed to such an extent that they were excellent means for the expression of his talent. The time when a person is born can make all the difference.

Many magnificent persons were born before the time of Christ, prophets like Isaiah and Jeremiah, kings like David and Solomon. And yet ordinary people like us have an unimaginable advantage over them. We live in the age of Jesus Christ. The time of our birth has made all the difference. The revelation of God's love and goodness in the words and deeds of Jesus Christ is the perfection for which the people of the Old Testament unconsciously yearned. Indeed through faith they could see God's love for them, especially in their freedom from slavery in Egypt, but they had no inkling that God so loved the world that he would send his own son as a savior. They could sense God's goodness in his care and concern for them as a people in their homeland, but they did not fully realize that God's goodness was so great that he has prepared an eternal homeland in heaven.

We should be amazed that God has given us being in this age of fullness, this age of Christ, and that he has put us in circumstances in which we have responded to his gift of faith. How grateful we should be, for we are truly more blessed than many prophets and kings!

WEDNESDAY OF THE FIRST WEEK

ISAIAH 25:6-10

In this passage the Lord is thanked and praised for what He will do on the day of judgment and blessing. On that day He will grant all men a seat at the eschatological banquet, giving them all the blessings that come with the establishment of His kingdom. Moreover, on that day He will destroy death and so remove from mankind the veil of mourning and wipe away their tears and remove the reproach of His people. Therefore, let all rejoice at this salvation which comes from the Lord and confess that it is the Lord who will do this according to His promise.

Reflection

Isaiah painted a picture of the great day of the Lord in images of a magnificent banquet: "a feast of rich food and choice wine." The splendid meal will be as joyful as it will be sumptuous, for "The Lord God will wipe away tears from all faces; he will destroy death forever."

In the Mass we have an image of the magnificent banquet of heaven. The image, however, is already the reality by anticipation. In the Mass the Lord provides for us, his people, not a feast of rich food and choice wines, but the spiritual nourishment of the body and blood of Jesus Christ. In the Mass the Lord wipes away the tears from our faces, for in the Eucharist, the sacrament of the death and resurrection of Jesus Christ, we have a guarantee of our own resurrection from the dead. Jesus said. "He who eats my flesh and drinks my blood has life eternal and I will raise him up on the last day" (Jn. 6:54). How fitting is our proclamation of the mystery of faith, "Dying you destroyed our death; rising you restored our life; Lord Jesus, come in glory."

For the Mass to mean what it should, our faith must be more than a proclamation on our lips. It must penetrate our whole beings and transform our entire outlook. Yes, real, deep faith is what we need—to see that whether the Mass is celebrated with the quiet simplicity of a weekday in our own church or amid the impressive splendor of a special feast in St. Peter's Basilica in Rome, it is the spiritual meal which anticipates the glory of eternal life. In every Mass we can say: "Behold our God, to whom we looked to save us! This is the Lord for whom we looked; let us rejoice and be glad that he has saved us!"

MATTHEW 15:29-37
> *Verses 29-31 form a transition from the healing of the daughter of the Canaanite woman (v. 21-28) to the feeding of the four thousand and are meant to explain how a crowd came to be with Jesus in a remote area. The crowd here is probably made up of Gentiles and so we are meant to see the cures of Jesus (intended to recall Is. 35:5-6) as a manifestation of Jesus bringing salvation to the Gentiles. The feeding of the four thousand is a duplicate of 14:13-21, with a few minor changes. Eucharistic formulas are used in verse 35 and so the story is meant to be a symbol and an anticipation of the Eucharistic celebration itself. Whereas the 5000 in 14:13-21 were Jews, here the 4000 probably are meant to be Gentiles who will also be saved by Christ and partake of the Eucharist.*

Reflection

The names of very few cities hold as much meaning for us as that of Bethlehem. That name calls to our minds images of Mary and Joseph bending in loving care over the newborn baby, of shepherds looking on in wonder and awe, and of angels singing their "Glory to God in the highest." And yet the greatest significance is found in the literal meaning of the word "Bethlehem" in Hebrew: "house of bread."

Among many ancient peoples bread was the fundamental source of nourishment and therefore a symbol of all the good things needed to sustain life. Even now we ourselves speak of a person who earns a living for his family as the "bread-winner." In today's gospel Jesus fed the people miraculously with bread. This miracle was a sign that he wanted to give all good things to us, that he wanted to give us a share in his own life of happiness. Jesus later made a promise. He said, "The bread that I will give is my flesh for the life of the world." He made good that promise at the Last Supper, and he continues to keep his promise in every Mass we celebrate.

Jesus was made flesh in the womb of Mary and born in Bethlehem, the "house of bread," so that he could give us his flesh as our spiritual bread. His birth was the turning point in history. How privileged was Mary to give birth to the child. How blessed was Joseph to share Mary's joy. How fortunate were the shepherds and the angels to witness the event. And yet we need not feel deprived. Though Bethlehem took place many centuries ago, its purpose is fulfilled whenever we receive the body of Jesus in communion as our church becomes a new Bethlehem, a house of spiritual bread.

THURSDAY OF THE FIRST WEEK

ISAIAH 26:1-6

This is an invitation to trust in the Lord under the guise of a processional liturgy. Jerusalem is praised for its strength which derives from its protection by the Lord (v. 1). Then comes a call to the gatekeepers to open the gates and let in the nation which is just and faithful to the Lord and which He keeps in peace because of its trust in Him (v. 2-3). Finally, there is the call to the people to trust in the Lord forever because He will always be their rock, their dependable source of protection and strength. Moreover He will humble the proud beneath the feet of the poor and needy, i.e., those who trust in Him.

Reflection

In today's lesson God warned through the prophet, Isaiah, that he would humble those in high places and tumble their city to the ground. The proud who thought they could get along without God were doomed to failure. On the other hand, God wanted his faithful to realize that they had to stand before him and profess that without his help they could not possibly make a true success of life. This spirit is summarized in today's responsorial psalm: "It is better to take refuge in the Lord than to trust in man; it is better to take refuge in the Lord than to trust in princes." Mary, the mother of Jesus, had this spirit of humility. When her cousin, Elizabeth, praised her for having been chosen to become the mother of Jesus, Mary took no credit for herself and gave none to any other human person. She responded to Elizabeth's praise by directing the praise to God: "My being proclaims the greatness of the Lord, and my spirit finds joy in God my savior, for he has looked upon his servant in her lowliness."

It is a foolish person who wants to be self-reliant or

who thinks he can depend only on other human beings to make life worthwhile. It is not that we are bad or that other human beings are bad. It's just that without God no one can make us happy. Turning to God and depending on him is the only realistic approach to life.

One of the great marvels of Christmas is that the eternal Son of God did not deem divinity something to cling to but humbled himself to come among us as a man. He chose to be as dependent on his Father in his humanity as we are in ours. That act of humility is the model for all of us.

MATTHEW 7:21, 24-27
> *These verses form part of the conclusion to Matthew's Sermon on the Mount. Simply calling upon the name of the Lord is not a sufficient response to the message of Christ. The desired response is the doing of God's will as this has been outlined in the Sermon. Failure to respond to the call to action in the Sermon will result in one's meeting destruction on the eschatological day of judgment. He will be like a man who builds his house on the sand of the wadi or river bed. When the torrents and winds of the eschatological testings come he will not be able to survive but be destroyed.*

Reflection

Christmas is favored with some of the most beautiful music ever composed. The marvelous carols we hear during this season help to put us in the right mood, to stir up within us the Christmas spirit whereby we really want to have good will toward all men. But a funny thing happens on December 26th. Abruptly all the carols come to an end. And usually, so does the Christmas spirit.

Jesus says, "None of those who cry out, 'Lord, Lord,' will enter the kingdom of God but only the one who does the will of my Father in heaven." Perhaps our singing of

Christmas songs is all too like crying out "Lord, Lord," without any persevering effort to carry out God's will in our lives. God's will is that we learn to live together as his children, as brothers and sisters, with love and concern for each other, with patience and acceptance. The feelings we have on Christmas day are good, but not enough. We must not build our religion upon a foundation of emotions alone. Emotions change, like shifting sand. God wants us to live together as his children all the time, not just when we are feeling good or when others are pleasant with us. We need the firm foundation of unrelenting, determined effort to be unselfish, to be generous with others—in a word, to be more like Christ himself.

During this time of Advent we need to think about how we treat others. We have to get serious about putting our religion of love into practice. We must devote more time to praying that God will help us to follow his will in our dealings with each other. Maybe then we can have Christmas every day this coming year.

FRIDAY OF THE FIRST WEEK

ISAIAH 29:17-24

> *The prophet had been berating Israel for her sinfulness and threatening chastisement. But now he speaks of the redemption that will follow. Verse 17 is probably an ancient proverb whose exact meaning is not known but the idea behind it is that God's redemption of His people will bring about a radical change. Those who had been blind to the ways of the Lord and deaf to His word (see v. 9f) will now see His work and hear His word. Moreover, the lowly and the poor will rejoice in the Lord because the evildoers, those who have wreaked injustice, will be destroyed. Also, the people will no longer have anything to be ashamed of since God will redeem them as He had redeemed*

> *Abraham in the past. Seeing God working in their midst they will give Him the reverence due Him. Finally, those who had erred in the past will now have a true understanding of God's will.*

Reflection

If we had to be deprived of one of our human faculties, I suspect that most of us would be least willing to give up our power of sight. The prospect of never again seeing the faces of those we love, the beauty of a Spring day, even a movie or television, is indeed frightening. We can close our eyes and try to imagine what it would be like to be totally blind—but of course all the while we know that we can simply open our eyes to see again.

The scriptures frequently present sinfulness in terms of blindness, and redemption in terms of seeing. In this context Isaiah wrote, "Out of gloom and darkness the eyes of the blind will see." Because of the coming of Jesus Christ we live in the age of redemption. In baptism our eyes were opened to see the Lord in faith. But do we keep our eyes open?

God is present for us to see everywhere, especially in people. His joy is in the smile of an infant. His acceptance of us is in the affection of a child. His vibrance is in the energy of an adolescent. His power is in the strength of an athlete. His beauty is in the loveliness of a young girl. His concern is in the devotion of a parent. His wisdom is in the prudence of the elderly. Every human person has something of the goodness of God within him. What a shame it is to close our eyes to God's presence, to live in darkness and gloom, when all we have to do is open our eyes in faith to see him.

MATTHEW 9:27-31

> *This miracle story is a doublet of* 20:29-34, *and another one of the ten miracles related in chapters* 8

and 9 *to show that the messianic era has arrived in Jesus. The whole structure of chapters 8-10 is governed by 11:2-6. Hence, Matthew has brought in this story here in order to have an example of the blind recovering their sight at the hands of Jesus. The point of the story itself is the demand for faith in Jesus as Lord if one wishes to be the recipient of the Lord's saving power.*

Reflection

These are days for dropping little hints about what we would like to get for Christmas. Even though it was not Christmas for the two blind men in the gospel, they left no doubt as to what they wanted. They were not satisfied with hints. They went crying after Jesus and begging him to have pity on them by giving them sight. Jesus granted their request in response to their faith.

We can consider ourselves fortunate if we do not have a need as great as that of the blind men. But we do have needs, and we like to think that we have faith as well. Imagine yourself, then, as being given the opportunity of asking God for anything you wanted. What would you ask for? What is the one great favor you would like to receive?

Frankly I find this question very difficult to answer. I can think of a thousand things to ask for, but one and only one . . . well, I am just not sure. Heaven? Yes, of course, I want to get to heaven. But that is probably still far away and there is a lot of living to do before I can get there. Should I pray for wisdom as did Solomon? Should I ask for the patience of Job or the charity of St. Vincent de Paul? Wait a minute! Wasn't Jesus himself the night before he died in a position of asking his Father for one thing? As Jesus knelt in the garden of Gethsemane his prayer was simple: "Not my will but yours be done." I could not have a better prayer, for that simple prayer includes everything. It expresses supreme faith in the power of God and complete hope and trust in his goodness. Above all it manifests real love. It is no wonder that Mary's prayer at the annunciation was so similar: "Be it done to me according to your word."

"Not my will but yours be done." How I must make that prayer my own.

SATURDAY OF THE FIRST WEEK

Isaiah 30:19-21, 23-26

Isaiah reassures the people of Jerusalem, who have just heard his threat of suffering because of their sins, that if in their suffering they will once again turn to the Lord and cry out to Him that He will answer them and be gracious towards them. At that time He will pour out His blessings upon them giving them all that they need for life and in some way He will speak directly to them showing them the right path to take to come to Him. On that day when the Lord destroys Israel's enemies all nature will be transformed to such an extent that even the animals will have only the best to eat. Moreover, the Lord Himself will bind up and heal the bruises His people have suffered because of the chastisement that He has sent upon them.

Reflection

Isaiah paints a picture of the goodness of God toward his people: "He will be gracious to you when you cry out. He will give you the bread you need. A voice shall sound in your ears: 'This is the way; walk in it.'" It is a beautiful picture of God's goodness, and it is a picture which comes to life in the Mass.

We approach God in the Mass by crying out to him,

"Lord, have mercy." That cry is more than a plea that God forgive our sins, for "mercy" includes all that we understand by the words "love" and "kindness." Our first prayer of the Mass is a request that God show us his concern and his guidance. God is then indeed gracious to us. He does not hide himself nor is he deaf to our prayer. Rather, he speaks to us in the words of sacred scripture. As we listen to the lesson and the gospel, we should realize that it is God's voice sounding in our ears and saying, "This is the way; walk in it."

God does not point out to us how we should live without giving us the strength needed to walk in his way. He feeds us with a bread more marvelous than the manna which came from heaven, more beneficial than any human nourishment, more joy-giving than the most sumptuous banquet. He gives us the Eucharist.

The Mass, however simply celebrated, is something we must never fail to appreciate. We should praise the Lord, for he is good to us. We should sing praise to our God, for he is gracious to us.

MATTHEW 9:35-10:1, 6-8

> *Verses 35-38 form the transition from the narrative material in chapters 8 and 9 to the missionary discourse of Jesus in chapter 10. The reason Jesus sends forth the Twelve is his compassion for the poor and ignorant, the people of the land, the spiritually unenlightened in the eyes of the Pharisees. To the Twelve, who are compared to laborers who gather the harvest, Jesus gives a share in his own power over evil and sends them forth as an extension of himself to aid him in his mission. They are to announce without charge the nearness of the kingdom and to demonstrate its nearness through healings and exorcisms just as Jesus was doing (cf. 10:7-8 and 9:35). The restriction of their mission to the Jews reflects the historical situation at the time of Jesus where the kingdom was first announced to the Jews. It was when*

they rejected it that the kingdom was then offered to the Gentiles.

Reflection

The scene in today's gospel is a touching one. The heart of Jesus was moved with pity for the crowds who were like sheep without a shepherd. God had sent Jesus into the world as his own special Gift to just such people, among whom we are numbered. We are so used to this picture of Jesus that we may fail to notice his final words in today's gospel: "The gift you have received, give as a gift."

God has favored us by giving us faith in Jesus. This gift, however, is not to be hoarded as if it were too precious to be shared with others. Faith is different from material things. If you give someone money, you necessarily have less yourself. If you give someone your faith, you not only do not have less, you actually have more. In fact, to grow in our Christian life we must share with others this most precious gift from God. We associate with people every day who do not enjoy our gift of faith. While we must respect their own personal convictions, we should never be reluctant to try to draw them to full faith in Jesus Christ by our words, our good example, our interest, our own obvious sense of conviction and dedication.

A five-year-old girl, an only child, received a whole carload of presents from her parents for Christmas. Her mother noticed, however, that she seemed strangely reserved and subdued as she played with some of her new toys. She asked her daughter, "Aren't you happy with what Santa Claus brought you?" "Yes," the little girl answered, "but I didn't give Santa Claus anything for Christmas." In her simplicity that child had caught a real meaning of Christmas and of Christianity itself. We should be grateful for our gifts from God, but we must learn to be givers as well as receivers.

MONDAY OF THE SECOND WEEK

ISAIAH 35:1-10
This section comes from after the time of Isaiah himself and is a report of a vision of what will take place when the Lord comes to save His people who are here pictured as being in Exile. At that time, because of the presence of the Lord, all of nature will be transformed and all human misery will be wiped out. Therefore, let the feeble, the weak and the frightened take heart for the Lord is coming to save them. Moreover, the Lord will make special preparations for their journey through the desert back to Jerusalem. He will see that there is abundant water for them and the road home will be kept free from the unclean and the beasts of prey. With great joy the redeemed will once again enter Jerusalem and all sorrow and mourning will disappear.

Reflection

Charles Dickens in his famous novel, *David Copperfield*, created a delightful character by the name of Wilkins Micawber who was forever in financial difficulty. He was alternately buoyed by the hope that at last fortune was to be his and reduced almost to despair by sudden, unaccountable reverses. And yet it is his optimism which readers remember since Mr. Micawber was constantly "looking for something to turn up."

Caricature though he is, Mr. Micawber is a reflection of the great prophets of the Old Testament. The prophets were at times reduced almost to despair because of the people's repeated infidelities to God and the consequences of those infidelities in war and destruction. And yet it is always their optimism which we should remember since the prophets were constantly "looking for something to turn up." That something was the Day of the Lord when all wrongs would be righted. Today's lesson is typical.

It was written during a bleak period in the history of God's people, a time of punishment in exile far from their homeland and their precious temple in Jerusalem. The prophets proclaimed a message of hope and encouagement to the people, the promise that the Lord would come.

The Day of the Lord arrived in the coming of Jesus Christ. But this "day" of the Lord was not a day of twenty-four hours nor was it a period of thirty-three years, for Jesus is still coming into our world. He is working even now to right the wrongs of the world through people who allow him to enter their lives. How long this day will last, we do not know. Whether we are still only at the dawn or have moved toward noon is uncertain. One thing is definite: despair is no part of the Christian outlook. "Something will turn up," and that something is the final coming of Christ when the Day of the Lord will reach its eternal zenith.

Luke 5:17-26

> *In this episode Jesus is presented as the one who has authority on earth to forgive sins. In the Jewish mind sin and sickness or deformity were closely connected since the Jews saw any sickness or deformity as being the result of sin. Hence, in the Jewish mind, Jesus, by curing any illness, manifests his power over its cause, sin. Jesus, then, is the one who fulfills Daniel's vision of the Son of Man who receives authority to exercise divine judgment (Dan. 7:13f). The response of the man who was healed and of the crowd should be the response of all Christians to these realities. In the context of the gospel of Luke this episode brings out one of the reasons for the conflict that grew up between Jesus and the Jewish leaders.*

Reflection

We tend to take words for granted since we speak and hear so many of them every day. In this gospel Jesus spoke human words which sounded no different from any other human words. And yet what a difference there was, for behind his human words was his divine power. Jesus proved the power of his words to forgive sins by showing that his words could cure physical paralysis. In the day of creation God said, "Let there be light," and there was light. In the day of salvation Jesus said, "Your sins are forgiven," and they were forgiven.

The words of Jesus are with us still. We hear them through the voice of a fellow human being, the priest, and yet behind those words is the divine power of Jesus himself. They are sacramental words—words such as "I absolve you from your sins" and "This is my body; this is my blood." No proof is given now along with the words as was the case for the paralytic. Ours is the gift of faith rather than the gift of physical healing.

During Advent we are preparing for our celebration of the coming of Jesus Christ into the world as a human being. The incarnation was a marvelous manifestation of God's love for us, and that incarnation is continued and extended through the sacraments, especially Penance and the Eucharist. We must never take sacramental words for granted. Instead we should be filled with awe and give praise to God by saying "We have seen and heard incredible things."

TUESDAY OF THE SECOND WEEK

Isaiah 40:1-11

> *Chapters 40-55 of Isaiah come from an unknown prophet who spoke about 150 years after Isaiah to the people of Israel in exile. This inaugural vision of the prophet places him in the presence of the heavenly court. There he hears God address His court (1-2) and declare that comfort is now to be extended to His*

people (Jerusalem) for He is about to lift the judgment He has imposed upon them. A member of the court then cries out that in accordance with the decree of the Lord everything is to be prepared for a new Exodus, for the glory of the Lord is about to be revealed to all men (3-5). This manifestation of God's glory is described in the announcement that Zion is to make to all the cities of Judah (8-11): the Lord will be seen delivering His people from exile and guiding them back to Jerusalem as a shepherd guiding His flock. Verses 6-11 stress the fact that this will take place because God has decreed it and man can do nothing to hinder it.

Reflection

A man driving from work was in a near-fatal accident. When his wife received the word she rushed to the hospital where he had been taken. A young intern informed her that her husband had received emergency treatment upon arrival and was now undergoing surgery. Though his condition was critical, he was still alive. The intern tried to comfort the wife by reminding her that where there is life, there is hope. The words struck the distressed woman as banal, as perhaps they would us in a similar situation. And yet the simple words, "Where there is life, there is hope," contain a profound truth.

Our world is in critical condition. It is near death because of war, social injustice, and pollution. Everything we try to do seems little better than emergency treatment, and there is small comfort in that. But the world is not dead, and where there is life, there is hope. Most important of all, a surgeon, a divine physican, is even now working to repair the serious injuries done to the world through sin, the real cause of all our ills. From time to time, as in today's first lesson, he sends a message to us, "Comfort, give comfort to my people." All will yet be well. Unlike the woman in the hospital we can do more than just wait.

Hope does not mean passivity. But at least just for this moment, let us realize that the hope we have is derived not from human activity, however important, but from God. To all the prophets of doom we should not fear to counter with the words of the prophet of hope and consolation: "Here is your God. Here comes with power the Lord God."

MATTHEW 18:12-14
> *In the context of the gospel it is clear that the point of this piece of instruction to the disciples is the responsibility of the shepherds of the Church for all those who believe ("the little ones"). The plan of the Father is that not a single believer shall ever come to grief. Hence, the disciples, who are to carry on the mission of Christ, have the responsibility to be concerned for all who believe in Jesus. Just as the shepherd has the responsibility to care for all his sheep and to go out and try to bring back any who may go astray, even if it is only one, the disciples also must try to bring back all who go astray.*

Reflection

Sometimes we say of a person whom we esteem that he is worth his weight in gold. That means a newly born baby would be valued at about four thousand dollars and a fully grown man at about one hundred thousand. According to this measure the president of the United States in a year's time is worth twice his weight in gold.

God, however, does not measure the worth of people according to monetary values; he is not on the gold standard. Rather his standard is the life of his son, for people have been redeemed not with perishable things, with silver or gold, but with the blood of Christ which is beyond all price (cf. 1 Pt. 1:18f). Jesus suggested that God is like a shepherd who values even one sheep so much that he leaves the ninety-nine to search for the one that is lost, for with God every human person is precious, even "little" people whom the "big" people of this world may despise. Grown men and babies, presidents and ordinary citizens are all valuable in the eyes of God.

In Advent we are thinking about God's sending his son as the redeemer of the human race. We should draw from our devotions a real respect and esteem for every human person without exception, big people and little people, black and white people, rich people and poor people. Don't measure anyone by your own standard. Use God's standard, the blood of his son which is beyond all price.

WEDNESDAY OF THE SECOND WEEK

Isaiah 40:25-31

Among the exiles there was a real despair, a sense of having been abandoned by God and even a lack of confidence in His power to save them. To counter this the prophet reminds the people that it was the Lord who alone had created the whole world and that there is no one equal to the Lord in strength and power. Even the stars, which their pagan masters worship, the Lord created simply by calling out their name and it is He who now guides their course through the heavens. Hence, these stars are not gods but the Lord alone is God, a God who is totally other from everything earthly (25-26). Therefore, let them not think that the Lord has forgotten them for He is not only the creator but the eternal God, i.e., the one who controls all that happens in time. He never grows weak but is the source of strength to all who trust in Him.

Reflection

In the earlier days of movies a cartoon was a regular part of the program in every theater. I remember seeing a cartoon in which a bear, before settling down for his hibernation, wound and set an alarm clock. The winter went by and at the selected time when the alarm sounded the clock went haywire, with hands and screws and springs flying wildly about. Through it all the bear continued to sleep soundly.

Some people seem to picture God to be like the bear in the cartoon, as if he created the world, wound it up and let it run all by itself. Now the world is indeed beginning to go haywire and they think that, despite the alarms sounded all around us, God is still asleep and completely unconcerned. Their only hope is that God will at last awaken and finally "intervene in human history" to set things right through a brilliant second coming of his son.

Today's lesson gives us a completely different picture of God. The Jewish exiles in Babylon to whom the lesson was addressed felt as if they had been abandoned by God. The prophet assured them that God by his great might and the strength of his power is always active in the world, that he never grows faint or weary and is aware of everything that is going on. The truth is that God's act of creation is continuous, and without his constant almighty power the entire universe would lapse into nothingness.

No, God is not asleep nor will the final coming of his son be a sudden "intervention," for God is without interruption actively in control of his creation, gently and wisely directing it to the goal of perfection in the second coming of his son, a plan he has had in mind all along.

MATTHEW 11:28-30

This passage, an invitation to follow Jesus, is addressed to those who find life weary and burdensome under the heavy yoke of the Law as explained by the scribes and Pharisees. Jesus promises that whoever submits himself to the kingdom of God through the acceptance of his message (a message of love and humility) will find peace of mind, for this message of Jesus gives to the believer an intimate knowledge of the

Father that makes it easy to live under His will (see v. 27). These three verses are the concluding part of a hymn found in verses 25-30 (for the first part of the hymn see Lk. 10:21-22: TUESDAY *of the* FIRST WEEK*).*

Reflection

You've had it happen to you. Something very serious has gone wrong and you are depressed. When a friend tries to cheer you up, your retort is: "It's fine for you to be so cheerful; you don't have my problem." And you turn away from your friend.

Jesus wants to be a friend to us. He invites us to come to him to find refreshment from the weariness brought on by all the burdens of life. We should never reject his invitation on the grounds that he does not understand our human situation. He has been through it all. In the mystery of the incarnation Jesus became as human as we are in everything except sin. His humanity was no fiction, no make-believe. The Vatican Council reminds us of this truth: "By his incarnation the Son of God has united himself in some fashion with every man. He worked with human hands, he thought with a human mind, acted by human choice, and loved with a human heart" (*Church in the Modern World*, 22).

Have you suffered the loss of a loved one? In his youth Jesus had to bury his foster father, Joseph, and later wept real tears before the tomb of his friend Lazarus. Are you plagued by bills and financial losses? Jesus assumed the obligation of caring for twelve apostles even though he had no place to lay his own head and frequently did not know where his next meal was coming from. Do you find that you lack peace and quiet, that people are always making demands on you and your time? Jesus had crowds of people following him and asking for all kinds of favors.

Has someone you loved and trusted turned his back on you and hurt your feelings? Jesus in his passion was betrayed by Judas, denied by Peter, and abandoned by the other apostles.

When Jesus says, "Come to me and I will refresh you," have no doubt that he understands your problems. He has been through it all.

THURSDAY OF THE SECOND WEEK

ISAIAH 41:13-20

The Lord has been reassuring His people that He is about to deliver them from their oppressors. Hence, Israel is not to fear any longer for He who is making these promises is the Lord, the one who redeemed them from Egypt long ago and who is about to deliver them once again. In fact the Lord will use Israel, who is like a worm when compared to her enemies who are like mountains, as His instrument of judgment to destroy her oppressors. Then, through the imagery of abundant water and a fertile desert, the Lord promises the needy and afflicted who have put their hopes in Him that He will answer their prayers and bless them, thus fulfilling his plan of salvation. He will do all this so that all may recognize that the Holy One of Israel has done what He had announced beforehand.

Reflection

The period of the Babylonian captivity was a difficult time for the Jews. Living conditions apparently were not as bad as in the previous Egyptian captivity, but the devout Jew missed the worship of the temple in Jerusalem and in a strange land he eventually felt abandoned by God. He was somewhat like a child who while playing with friends has wandered a little too far from home. As it begins to get dark the child suddenly realizes that he is lost, and his only thought through all his fears and anxieties is to get back home. Then he looks up and sees his father coming toward him. He rushes gratefully into his open arms, and hand in hand the two make their way home.

God, the Father of his people, said to them in exile: "I am the Lord, your God, who grasp your right hand; it is I who say to you, 'Fear not, I will help you.'" And God says the very same thing to us today. We have here no lasting city but we look for the city that is to come (Heb. 13:14). In this life we are exiled from the Lord (2 Cor. 5:6). We should not be surprised if at times our world appears dark and we experience a sense of being lost, of being all alone. The world is good and people are good, but God is our Father and heaven is our home. All human groping for happiness is ultimately a search for God and as St. Augustine said, our hearts will be restless until they rest in God.

God wants to lead us home. Through all the dark, lonely days of life we need to pray for faith—a faith that will open our ears to hear the consoling words of a Father: "I am the Lord, your God, who grasp your right hand; it is I who say to you, 'Fear not, I will help you.'"

MATTHEW 11:11-15
> *The point of this pericope is the contrast between the period of the Law and the prophets and the period of the kingdom. The period of the Law and the prophets is represented by John who as the last of the prophets and the promised forerunner who announces the coming of the kingdom spoken of in Malachi 3:1, 22, is the greatest figure of this period. Yet, whoever is a member of the kingdom of God is greater than him. Here we see the greatness and all-importance of the kingdom. The meaning of verse 12 is not clear. In the context it would seem best to take it as meaning that through Jesus the kingdom is making a vio-*

lent entrance into the world and it is those who are ready to be violent, i.e., those who are ready to carry out Jesus' message, who will gain entrance into the kingdom.

Reflection

Evil cannot tolerate good because it sees good as a threat. John the Baptist preached repentance in an attempt to turn people back to God, but Herod saw him as a personal denunciation of his depraved life and beheaded him. Jesus proclaimed a kingdom of love and peace, but the Pharisees viewed him as an exposer of their corrupt religious leadership and conspired to put him to death. And so through the long history of the Church men and women have paid with their lives for their commitment to the goodness of Jesus Christ. Evil correctly views good as a threat, for the two are quite incompatible.

Jesus warned that the kingdom of God suffers violence, for it is good confronting evil. But then Jesus added an enigma: "the violent take it by force." The meaning of these obscure words seems to be that evil must be met with resistance, and that only those who are brave enough to engage evil in a life and death struggle can become part of his kingdom. Passivity on the part of good leads only to victory for evil.

We are mistaken, however, if we think that the struggle between good and evil is going on only outside us. The real battle is within. Each one of us contains something of good and something of evil. We must come to grips with the fact that it is difficult to be a follower of Jesus Christ. Do we really listen to the teaching of Jesus Christ or do we dismiss it as impractical or irrelevant or as directed to others but not to us? His teaching, remember, is a threat to our complacency, our selfishness, and our laziness. To follow his teaching we must be willing to do violence to ourselves. Otherwise we will find to our regret that passivity has led to a victory for evil.

FRIDAY OF THE SECOND WEEK

Isaiah 48:17-19

> Here we find an appeal to Israel by God to keep the commandments which He gave them at Sinai. He gave them to her for her good so that she might know and follow the way to salvation. Implied here is the accusation of past disobedience as the cause for her present suffering in exile. But if she will but be faithful to these commandments now the Lord will never forget her or abandon her but bless her abundantly. It should be noted here that the prophet who is responsible for chapters 40-55 of the book of Isaiah normally stresses God's action in the salvation of Israel. What this passage brings out, however, is that if God's act of salvation is to be effective Israel must cooperate by keeping the commandments.

Reflection

An important duty of parents is to teach their children to talk. In the long, laborious process, there is one word which every child seems to learn all by himself, a word which no one has to teach him. And that one word is "no." There are many things most children say "no" to, such as eating the right kind of food and going to bed at the proper time. It would be the easiest thing in the world for parents simply to allow a child to do whatever he wants—no more tears and no more pouting. Such peace! But complete permissiveness is in no way a sign of love. Parents who do not take the time and effort to guide their children have abandoned their role and are not worthy to have children under their care. Children cannot be expected to know what is good for them. Parents have the right and duty to discipline their children because they are wiser and more experienced.

God is infinitely wise and his experience is eternal. His love is without measure. That is why he can and does say, "I, the Lord, your God, teach you what is for your good, and lead you on the way you should go." No matter how old we may be, in relation to God we are like children. Without his guidance we would be worse off than a little child trying to grow up without parents. Ignoring God's commandments can only make a shambles of our lives. This was the bitter lesson the Jews had to learn, for their period of exile was the result of their disobedience.

We should be grateful to God that he loves us enough to take the time and effort to guide us through life by means of his commandments. The biggest mistake we can make is to say "no" to God.

MATTHEW 11:16-19

> *John and Jesus followed different life styles but neither one of them found real acceptance among the Jews. Jesus compares the Jews to bad-tempered, peevish children who are not satisfied with anything and find fault with everything. Yet, in time God's wisdom in working in the different ways that he has through John and Jesus will be justified by the fact that many will believe and answer the call to repentance issued by John and Jesus.*

Reflection

Abraham Lincoln said that you cannot fool all of the people all of the time. He could just as correctly have said that you cannot please all of the people any of the time. John the Baptist led an austere life and preached repentance, so some people dismissed him as a fanatic. Jesus lived in a normal fashion and proclaimed God's merciful love for everyone, and they accused him of being a laxist.

Much the same sort of thing is going on today. Some say that the Church since Vatican II has moved too fast, others that it has moved too slowly. Some maintain that the Church has abandoned her role as a moral guide, others that the Church is still bogged down in legalism. Some want to return to the past, and others feel that we haven't yet moved into the present. How true it is that you cannot please all of the people any of the time!

There is no simple solution to this problem. The Church is our concern, and every Catholic has a right to work for what he thinks should be changed or restored in the Church. But concern is not enough. The Bible says that God made man in his own image and likeness, and he did the same with his Church. We are in grave error if we attempt to reverse the process. It is God's will we must seek, not our own; his plan we must strive to follow, not our own.

We need humility and docility. For every word of criticism we have uttered, how many prayers have we addressed to God for guidance? For every moment of discontent, how often have we placed ourselves in the hands of God and said, "Your will be done"? Our real concern should be to please God all of the time.

SATURDAY OF THE SECOND WEEK

SIRACH 48:1-4, 9-11

This praise of the prophet Elijah is taken from that section of the book of Sirach called "The Praise of the Fathers." The purpose of this section is to show that true wisdom is found only in Israel and that the Israelites do not need to turn to Hellenism for such wisdom. The author achieves his purpose by simply recalling the lives of great men from Israel's past. Elijah is brought in as a reminder of the destruction that awaits those who turn against the Lord. The reference in verses 1-4 are to 1 Kings 17-18 and 2 Kings 1:9-14. In 2 Kings 2:11, the belief was expressed that Elijah was taken up to God in some marvelous way at the end of his life instead of dying. It was this belief which led the people to believe that he would come again, before the Lord appeared in judgment, to prepare the way of the Lord (see Mal. 3:1-23; Mt. 17:10f).

Reflection

Elijah was a great prophet extraordinarily favored by the Lord. It was believed that he did not die but was taken up to God at the end of his earthly life in some marvelous fashion. This belief led to a tradition that Elijah would appear again on this earth before the coming of the Messiah. According to the New Testament Elijah did appear again in the person of John the Baptist. This teaching does not reflect a belief in reincarnation; rather, it makes clear that the purpose of Elijah's prophetic office was fulfilled by the mission of the Baptist as he prepared the people to receive Jesus Christ.

In this sense we could correctly maintain that all the prophets of the Old Testament made a new appearance on this earth when John began his preaching, for the entire Old Testament era was intended to get the world ready for Christ. The future coming of the savior was proclaimed by all the prophets. We spend a few weeks preparing for the celebration of Christmas, but God dedicated centuries to his preparations. Throughout the long history of salvation in the Old Testament God was at work, patiently and wisely directing events toward the marvelous moment when his son would be one of us. When Jesus humbled himself to come among us as a man, he fulfilled the plan God formed long ago and opened for us the way to salvation (ADVENT PREFACE I).

Our preparation for Christmas is short in comparison with God's. That is why we must try to be as intense about it as possible. Daily Mass is an excellent means if we listen attentively to the readings and use them as a motive for giving thanks and praise to God in the Eucharist. When Christ comes at Christmas he should find us watching in prayer, our hearts filled with wonder and praise (ADVENT PREFACE II).

MATTHEW 17:10-13
> *In the context of the gospel of Matthew the point of this passage is that just as John the Baptizer was not recognized for what he was and was put to death so Jesus, the Son of Man, the Messiah, will also not be recognized for what he really is and be made to suffer. The dialogue itself has been deeply affected by post-resurrection controversies between Jews and Christians over the traditional messianic signs. Specifically, the Jews probably asked how the Christians would explain the tradition that Elijah had to come first (see Mal. 3:1-22) if Jesus was the Messiah. The answer the Christians gave, which is here shown to come from Christ, was that John the Baptizer had carried out this Elijan mission. So Matthew, then, understood that Elijah was to come as the forerunner of the Messiah (but see* FIRST READING *on* DECEMBER 23).

Reflection

Some high school students were decorating their school auditorium in preparation for a Christmas celebration. Since the crucifix did not seem appropriate for the season, they were thinking of removing it from the wall when one of their teachers, a priest, walked in. The priest urged them to allow the crucifix to remain. "After all," he said, "that is why Jesus was born—to die on the cross."

It was a point Jesus himself had to make. The episode in today's gospel occurred just after the transfiguration wherein Jesus gave three of his apostles a preview of the glory that would come to him in his resurrection. The transfiguration was intended to prepare them for the ordeal of the passion which would be a supreme test of faith for all the followers of Jesus. Jesus appreciated how difficult it would be for them to accept the fact of his death, and so he took the occasion of their question about Elijah to emphasize once again the necessity of his death. The second coming of Elijah was realized in the person of John the Baptist, a man who went unrecognized by the Jewish leaders and who was put to death. And Jesus added, "The Son of Man will suffer at their hands in the same way." In God's plan the evil action of men would be the means of achieving the glorification of his son and the salvation of the world.

For those who fail to recognize the true meaning of Christmas, the crucifix may seem out of place, but it is not. Jesus was born to die. Let the crucifix remain. It is a sign, not of ignominy, but of glory.

MONDAY OF THE THIRD WEEK

NUMBERS 24:2-7, 15-17

Balak, king of Moab, was frightened when Israel, on their way to the promised land, encamped in his country. He was afraid that the Israelites might take over his country. So he sent for Balaam, a seer, to come and lay a curse upon Israel so that disaster would befall them. After some hesitancy Balaam agreed to come but warned that he would speak only what the Lord would tell him to speak. But everytime that he tried to curse Israel the Lord put blessings in his mouth. Verses 2-7 are part of the third oracle of Balaam. He praises the goodness of Israel and promises blessings for them and foretells the greatness of their royalty (the reference is to David). Balak then dismisses Balaam but before Balaam goes he announces to Balak a great king will arise in Israel (David) who will crush Moab (15-17).

Reflection

When the Israelites were about to pass through Moab on their way from Egypt to the promised land, Balak, the Moabite king, feared that they would take over his country. He commissioned Balaam, a pagan diviner or seer, to curse the Israelites and render them powerless, but God would not permit Balaam even to utter the words of the curse. Four times he made the attempt, but on each occasion his words turned into a blessing. A person does not usually like to have someone put words in his mouth, but that is what happened to Balaam. Today's lesson summarizes two of his oracles.

The Balaam incident symbolizes God's providential care of his people and the fact that salvation comes from his power alone and not from any human resources. By all odds the Israelites should have vanished from the earth long before the coming of the Messiah. Apart from the golden era of David and Solomon, their history was generally marked by religious infidelities and military defeats culminating in the destruction of Jerusalem by the Babylonians in 587 B.C. Living in a tiny land, bereft of many natural resources and surrounded by powerful and hostile neighbors, the Jews were the last people that human wisdom would have chosen as the source of the Messiah-King. Only God had power to lead Israel to its fulfillment in the coming of Jesus Christ.

God's ways are not our ways. The Church, the New

Israel, has survived for twenty centuries. It began in Jerusalem with a small band, for the most part simple, unassuming people. From there it has spread over all the world. At times the Church has been rich and influential, at times poor and persecuted. Through it all the power of God has been at work, despite human weakness and corruption, and his power alone will bring the Church to its true golden age in the second coming of Jesus Christ.

MATTHEW 21:23-27

> *The Jewish leaders approach Jesus while he is teaching in the temple precincts and ask him on what authority he is doing this, i.e., where does his commission come from that gives him the right to teach in the temple precincts. Jesus counters with a question about the origin of John the Baptizer's commission. Out of their self-righteousness the Jewish leaders refuse to admit that John's commission was divine. Therefore, Jesus refuses to tell them the origin of his commission, for if they would not admit John's commission as divine they would not accept his as being divine either. It takes faith to understand who Jesus is. So the point of the episode is that the blindness of the Jewish leaders sprang from their self-righteousness. The consequences of this we see in the following episode (see* TUESDAY *of the* THIRD WEEK*).*

Reflection

At first glance the objection voiced by the Jewish leaders in today's gospel seems reasonable enough. Jesus had just driven from the temple those engaged there in buying and selling, and was now teaching in the temple precincts. In the eyes of the Jewish leaders Jesus was no more than an itinerant preacher, and they demanded to know by what authority he was interfering in the activities of the temple. What is a little surprising is that Jesus, rather than offering an explanation, chose to embarrass them with his question about the Baptist and then refused to answer their demand.

The Jewish leaders were the only people with whom Jesus was abrupt and even harsh at times. Since they had closed their eyes to what he had done, Jesus knew that they would close their ears to anything he would say. They of all people should have been able to read the meaning of the signs Jesus worked, signs which fulfilled the prophecies of the Old Testament in which they professed to be experts. They just could not bring themselves to believe that God was at work in this ordinary, untutored carpenter from Nazareth. They had blinded themselves by their smugness.

The marvel of Christmas is that God comes to us in the flesh of a baby. He continues to come to us in the unpretentiousness—one is tempted to say the plainness—of the Eucharist. Only faith can see through the veils of the humanity of Jesus, and only faith can see beyond the appearances of bread and wine. But faith is not for the smug, the sophisticated, the self-reliant. It is for those who are willing to respond to the wonderful simplicity of God's almighty power at work among us.

TUESDAY OF THE THIRD WEEK

ZEPHANIAH 3:1-2, 9-13

Zephaniah threatens the city of Jerusalem with punishment because of the sinfulness of her inhabitants. They are practicing social injustice, following after other gods and refusing to put their trust in the Lord and to accept His words of correction (1-2). But after the Lord will have punished all the nations for their sins (v. 8) things will be different. For He Himself will bring about the conversion of all the nations, and people from the north and the south will come to

Jerusalem to worship Him (9-10). *Moreover, after that day of woe the city of Jerusalem will no longer have to be ashamed of its past infidelities for the Lord will have destroyed the proud who would not listen to Him and those who remain will be the humble, those who have trusted in the Lord. They shall now live in peace and prosperity.*

Reflection

Zephaniah's prophecy sounds as if it were addressed to modern America with its problems of riots and ecology: "Woe to the city, rebellious and polluted. . . ." The prophet, however, had in mind something even more serious than the rebellion expressed in riots, for the people in turning to the worship of false deities were guilty of rebellion against the one true God. He protested against a situation more devastating than pollution of the environment, for the people had polluted their own minds and hearts, and the smog of selfishness had obscured their vision of God's commandments concerning love for others. With their abandonment of God came grave social injustices.

Is Zephaniah's prophecy addressed to us? We profess the true religion and we worship the one God as our regular participation in Mass gives witness. So the answer seems to be no. Religion, however, is not confined to church. St. Augustine wrote: "The perfection of religion is to imitate the One you worship."* God is made present to us in Jesus Christ, and our religion means imitating him. Did not Jesus show love and care for all without exception? Did he not resist the social evils of his day?

The means employed by some demonstrators these days is more than questionable, but maybe we condemn their means as a way of justifying our own complacency and inaction. Political and social questions are admittedly

---

* *De Civitate Dei*, VIII, 17.

complex, but perhaps we use complexity as an excuse for turning off a priest who from the pulpit is disturbing our conscience.

If we think religion means no more than coming to church, we are living in a polluting smog which is obscuring our vision of what God intends. "The perfection of religion is to imitate the One you worship." A question we all must ask ourselves is: "What would Jesus do in my situation?"

MATTHEW 21:28-32

> *The consequences of the stubborn self-righteousness of the Jewish leaders is now brought out. Because they had refused to put their faith in the divine missions of John and Jesus and repent, even though they professed allegiance to God, the despised tax collectors and prostitutes would push them out of the way and enter the kingdom of God before them. The point of the parable is the contrast between those who profess obedience and then disobey and those who at first profess disobedience and then obey. Jesus applies these two types to the Jewish leaders and the tax collectors and prostitutes respectively. One is saved only if he does what he is asked which is to have faith and repent.*

Reflection

When Jesus taught the people, he liked to take something of their experience as his starting point. He talked about sheep and coins and farmers. In today's gospel, in speaking about two sons, he drew from his own experience. Jesus, we must remember, is God's son. Each of the two young men he spoke about was like Jesus and unlike him. The elder was like Jesus in that he readily agreed to do what his father asked of him, and he was unlike him in that he failed to carry out his father's will. The younger was unlike Jesus in his initial refusal, and he was like him in his subsequent obedience.

It is obvious that Jesus approved of the younger son, the one who at first refused but later obeyed. Actions count, not words. Jesus also sympathized with the younger son. He knew how the boy felt. Though Jesus himself agreed to do his Father's will, it was a human struggle for him to accept his passion and cross. In the Garden of Gethsemane, when it was perfectly clear what his Father would ask of him on the next day, Jesus prayed, "My Father, if it is possible, let this cup pass me by." The prospect of having to die on the cross for the salvation of the world was not easy to accept. As a human being Jesus, like us, would have preferred a way out. But Jesus quickly added, "Still, let it be as you would have it, not as I" (Mt. 26:39). And the next day, opening his arms on the cross, he freely accepted death.

I personally feel that we should not be discouraged if at times of crisis we find a wave of rebellion surging within ourselves. Our first response cannot always be the best. Our actions, however, show what we are. That is why Jesus did not stop at teaching us to say, "Thy will be done." He also gave us a perfect example of accepting God's will. We should hope and pray that we will never say to God, "No, I will not," and yet the more important thing is not what we say but what we do.

WEDNESDAY OF THE THIRD WEEK

ISAIAH 45:6-8, 18, 21-25
> *The Lectionary here has gathered together several verses which have the common theme of the uniqueness of Yahweh, the God of Israel. In these verses the Lord declares that He alone is God and that there is no other. For it is He alone who has created light*

and darkness, happiness and even suffering. It is he alone who will bring the salvation prayed for by Israel. He it is who has created the heavens and the earth and put order in them. Therefore, all nations are invited to come and declare who it was that announced the salvation of Israel. The answer is that it was the Lord through His prophets. Hence, it must be clear that He alone is the God who saves. Therefore, all nations should turn to Him for protection and worship Him alone and declare that salvation is found in Him alone.

Reflection

The Israelites were surrounded by pagans who worshipped creatures, such as the moon and the stars or even rocks and trees. The chosen people stood out as unique in their belief in one Supreme Being, the Lord and Master of all creation. Their belief was not born of human instincts or superstitions, but was a gift of God's personal revelation of himself to his beloved people. Despite this revelation the people frequently drifted into the idolatry of their neighbors, and the prophets had to constantly call them back to the worship of the one true God.

Belief in one Supreme Being is so much a part both of our Catholic faith and our Western Civilization that we generally look upon worshippers of idols as being primitive and unsophisticated people. How unnecessary it seems for the creator of the heavens, the maker and designer of the earth, to protest to intelligent people: "I am the Lord and there is no other." The fact is, however, that we ourselves are surrounded by pagans who worship idols, pagans who exercise a considerable influence on us. Their idols are money, prestige, power, success, glamor. . . . The list could go on and on, but I suppose it could be summed up in one word: selfishness. "What's in it for me?" is more than an often repeated question. It is the expression of a form of religion.

Christmas reveals to us the goodness and love of God. Its message, like the proclamation of a modern prophet amid the allurements of idolatry, calls us from selfishness to a renewal of the worship of the one true God, who alone is worthy of a complete and total dedication.

Luke 7:18-23
> *Jesus is here presented as the one in whom is fulfilled the promises of what would take place when God comes to deliver His people (Is. 29:18-19; 35: 5-6; 61:1). John, who is in prison, has heard about Jesus' ministry and for some reason has begun to wonder if Jesus really is "He who is to come" after all. The title "He who is to come" is derived from Malachi 3:1-23 (see December 23). Jesus does not answer the question directly but asks John to make up his own mind by considering what he is doing in terms of Isaiah's promise concerning the time of God's deliverance of His people. In the light of what follows in the Gospel (7:24-28) Jesus is here pointing out that he is not the messenger of Malachi 3:1-23, but that he is rather the one through whom God is intervening in the world.*

Reflection

They say that you can know a man by the company he keeps. In that case Jesus gave rather surprising credentials for himself. Really you would expect a king, for such was Jesus, to hobnob with the wealthy, influential people of his day, and yet Jesus claimed as his intimates the poor, the blind, the cripples, and the lepers: people whom few would esteem as friends and whom many would not even want to be bothered with.

When Jesus came into our world as the long awaited Messiah-King, he did not look for his own comfort and pleasure either in the way in which he lived or in choosing to associate only with people who were pleasant and could return favors. He was born poor, he lived poor, and he died poor. The kind of people he most frequently associated with were those who needed him and who put something of a burden on him, people without any means of returning favors.

If Christmas is going to mean something to us this year, we must try through its celebration to become more like Jesus. It is true that we need friends who are agreeable and helpful to us; even Jesus had special friends. And in this sense charity begins at home, but it only *begins* there. Our love and concern must spread beyond a small circle of companions. We cannot treat everyone in the same way, but we must not deliberately exclude anyone from our love and respect, whether it be because of his color, his religion, his nationality, or just plain old orneriness. In fact, if we want to be more like Jesus, the "undesirables" of this world have a special claim on us.

When Jesus comes again I wonder if he will know us as his disciples by the company we keep.

THURSDAY OF THE THIRD WEEK

Isaiah 54:1-10

The exile was a rupture in the relationship between God and His people. As a result Israel was like a barren woman (v. 1), a widow (v. 4), a deserted wife (v. 6). But now Israel is to rejoice for the Lord is about to take her back and once again make her His wife and give her numerous offspring extending her reign over all the nations and take away the reproach of her widowhood. She is to forget the shame of her youth, i.e., her past sins. In verses 7-10, the central verses, the Lord explains that for a while He aban-

doned her out of anger over her sins. But because of His enduring love for her which springs from the fact that He was her Maker, her redeemer, and especially her husband (v. 5), He is now taking her back. He swears that His love for her will never again leave her just as He swore to Noah to never again destroy the earth by a flood (Gn. 9:15).

Reflection

God is love, and in his revelation God has been at pains to make it clear that he wishes to share his love, himself, with his people. One of the most beautiful images used for this purpose in the Old Testament is that which presents God and his people as husband and wife. As with human marriages, however, the relationship was not always ideal. Today's reading, addressed to the people in exile, takes on a particularly human quality wherein God admits, "For a brief moment I abandoned you (the period of exile) but with great tenderness I will take you back." God's love is so deep that despite the repeated "adulteries" of his spouse he cannot bring himself to divorce her.

The greatest expression of divine love was reached in the coming of Jesus Christ. Jesus entered into a new covenant, a new marital relationship, not with the chosen people alone but with the entire human race. Usually for a wedding the groom is dressed elegantly and his bride is attired in a beautiful gown. The marriage is sealed through the exchange of consent in a nervous but joyful atmosphere. The wedding of Jesus Christ and his people was unique. The groom hung naked upon a cross, his body battered and bloody. His bride was robed in the ugliness of sin. The marriage was sealed in the blood of Jesus. This ceremony, despite its outward appearances, was a profoundly glorious event, for the blood of Jesus was the sign of faithful, total love. "Christ gave himself up for his bride to make her holy and immaculate without stain or wrinkle" (Ep. 5:25f).

Even with all our imperfections Jesus Christ loves us more than any husband has ever loved his wife, and he himself will make us beautiful and attractive. He could not have taken greater pains to show his love for us.

LUKE 7:24-30

> *In the preceding passage (see* WEDNESDAY *of* THIRD WEEK) *Jesus had described himself in terms taken from Isaiah and had pointed out that God was intervening in the world through him to save man. Now he tells us who John is: he is the messenger promised by Malachi 3:1 who would prepare people for the coming of God to save man. John, then, may have been a great prophet but he belonged to the old age and was not a member of the Kingdom. With Jesus and his announcement of the Kingdom, the Kingdom has entered the world and anyone who is a member of the Kingdom is greater than John. That John had prepared the way for Jesus is now brought out by showing that those who had received John's baptism listened to Jesus and praised God. Not so those who had refused John's baptism (vv. 29-30).*

Reflection

John the Baptist was a person of austere virtue, an outstanding prophet, even a martyr. I find it difficult to think of myself as greater than this man, and yet Jesus assures us that the least born into the kingdom of God is greater than he. The point of comparison is the kind of birth one has, and therein lies the explanation of Jesus' remarkable statement.

John's birth was extraordinary in that his father was very elderly and his mother long past her childbearing years, but John as born of a woman is no match for one born of water and the Holy Spirit (Jn. 3:3ff). Through the birth of baptism we are born into the kingdom of God. That birth is a marvelous, mysterious introduction into the family of God, a sharing in his own divine life, the source of a new people.

The words of Jesus in today's gospel have the ring of finality. They proclaim the end of an epoch and the beginning of the last era of the world. All that has transpired in the Old Testament period, a period summed up in the person of John the Baptist, is fulfilled in the kingdom of Jesus Christ. John, great though he was, belonged to the old age. We, simple though we may be, have been born into the new kingdom. And that has made all the difference.

FRIDAY OF THE THIRD WEEK

ISAIAH 56:1-3, 6-8

>*In these opening verses of the third part of Isaiah, which is post-exilic, we find an invitation to obedience, a call to do what is right and just before the Lord, for God's salvation of man is about to be revealed. The man who is obedient, keeps the Sabbath and avoids all evildoing, will be happy for he will be the recipient of God's salvation. Moreover; the prophet insists that no one is to be excluded from the people of God, not even those non-Jews who live outside the boundaries of Palestine. Even these people will be accepted in the House of God and their sacrifices and prayers will be acceptable to the Lord if they but love the Lord, serve Him and keep the covenant. For the House of the Lord is "a house of prayer for all peoples." Finally, the Lord promises to gather together once again all those Israelites who have been dispersed.*

Reflection

Some Old Testament people developed a spirit of exclusiveness whereby they believed that only Jews could be saved. Isaiah in today's lesson made it clear that no one is excluded from God's favor, not even non-Jews living outside Palestine. In this spirit of Isaiah theologians are giving renewed emphasis to the mercy of God who wills the salvation of all men, an emphasis which gained approval in the Second Vatican Council. As a result, some Catholics are wondering what is the use of trying to win converts, or of trying to be a good Catholic, since God does indeed will the salvation of everyone.

The point is that religion is concerned not only with salvation in the future, of giving some guarantee of getting into heaven. Religion is also concerned with salvation here and now, which means leading people to achieve the real purpose of human existence in this life. The teachings of Jesus and the grace he won are intended to give us direction and help to live life to the full on this earth, as well as in heaven.

God wants all human beings to be now what they should be: people who worship him as their Father and who love one another as brothers and sisters. We still need a zeal that will move us to draw all men to Jesus Christ in his Church. The Second Vatican Council pointed out that good example is very important but that even more is required, for a true Christian "looks for opportunities to announce Christ by words addressed either to nonbelievers with a view of leading them to faith, or to believers with a view to instructing and strengthening them and motivating them toward a more fervent life" (*Decree on the Laity*, 6).

We should want to make the Church a house of prayer for *all* peoples.

JOHN 5:33-36
> *In 5:17-30 Jesus has claimed that it is he, the Son, who gives life and judges and by this has identified himself with the Father. According to the legal principle that a man is not to be believed on his own authority (v. 31) Jesus must now produce witnesses to the truth of his statement. Today's reading presents two of the four witnesses he brings forth (vv. 33-40) but all of these are only different aspects of the witness of "Another," i.e., the Father (v. 32). First there is John the Baptist; the Jews had admitted that John was from God and he had witnessed to Jesus (1:19-27). It is not that Jesus needs such human witnesses but he uses them in order that others might believe and be saved. Secondly, there are his miracles; they show he is from God for they could only have been given to him by the Father.*

Reflection

Jesus had spoken of God as his own Father, thereby making himself God's equal (Jn. 5:18). His claim had not gone unchallenged by his enemies. In response Jesus asserted that he could bring forth witnesses, John the Baptist for one, but more importantly he had recourse to a truth which we ourselves accept: actions speak louder than words. And so Jesus stated: "I have testimony greater than John's, namely, the works the Father has given me to accomplish." His works, especially his miracles, could have come from God alone.

At Christmas we profess our faith that the baby born of Mary in Bethlehem had only God as his Father. That belief is fundamental to Christianity, and without it Christmas would be little different from our celebration of Washington's birthday. Some say that Jesus was only a social reformer, a religious philosopher, a great humanist. Jesus is actually none of these things. A social reformer struggles to find a way to right the wrongs of the day, but Jesus is himself the Way that we all must follow. A religious philosopher seeks to discover and contemplate the truth about God, but Jesus is himself the Truth that we must discover and contemplate. A humanist values and celebrates life and all its goodness, but Jesus is himself the Life that can bring goodness to us. Jesus, being God, is the Way, the Truth, and the Life (Jn. 14:6).

Without Jesus any path a person follows simply goes around in circles. Without Jesus any search for truth becomes engulfed in darkness and confusion. Without Jesus even the longest and best life must come to an end. With Jesus we have a sure way to happiness, we find the truth that can set us free, and we enjoy the life that will last forever.

No readings are listed in the lectionary for a SATURDAY *of the* THIRD WEEK *of Advent since this day is always replaced by one of the days beginning on December 17.*

PART TWO

December 17ᵀᴴ--24ᵀᴴ

UNTIL HE COMES

DECEMBER 17

GENESIS 49:2, 8-10

Jacob's testament concerning the fate of his sons (49:1-27) is made up of several distinct oracles which mainly come from the period of the Judges and which were collected and put together in the time of David or Solomon. The situation presupposed is the tribal confederacy during the period of the Judges. The purpose of the whole seems to be to show that the later history of the twelve tribes was rooted in the history of the Patriarchs. The section on Judah probably dates from the period of David because its whole center of interest is David who came from this tribe. Here it is forecast that all the tribes will submit themselves to Judah (David) who is praised for his prowess in war. In spite of the textual problems in verse 10 the sense is clear enough: the reign of David and his seed will be permanent.

Reflection

When Jesus Christ was born, the Jews were a tiny, insignificant province within the mighty empire of Rome. From a human standpoint it would have made more sense for God to have chosen another people as the source of the Messiah-King—the Assyrians when their armies were all powerful, the Greeks when their philosophical wisdom was at its height, or the Romans of the day with their genius for law and government. But God knew what he wanted. He chose the tribe of Judah, the Jews, and from within that tribe he selected the house of David. He insisted that through David and his descendants the scepter, the ruling power, would never depart from Judah. In an eminent degree the prophecy of today's lesson was fulfilled in the person of Jesus Christ, born of the house of David as the Messiah-King.

God not only knew what he wanted; he also knew what he was doing. He was making it clear that he alone is God. He does not have to rely on mighty armies to conquer evil in the world. He does not have to appeal to philosophical wisdom for the spread of his truth. He does not have to rely on any human government to bring about justice and peace. God made his saving power present in a Jewish infant, Jesus Christ—an act which appears to be folly in the eyes of the wise of this world. He chose to pour out that salvation upon mankind through the blood of Christ poured out on the cross—an act which seems to be weakness in the eyes of the powerful of this world. God did what he did as a sign that we attain salvation, not by our own human efforts, but by his free gift in Jesus Christ.

No human wisdom, no human force can be given credit in place of God. It is right and just that we should give all the praise to God alone for the work of our salvation.

MATTHEW 1:1-17

Matthew is very concerned throughout his gospel to show that Jesus is the fulfillment of all the promises of the Old Testament. He brings this out very clearly here in the beginning of his gospel by presenting Jesus as the son of Abraham and the son of David. As the son of Abraham he is the one through whom all the nations of the earth will be blessed (Gn. 12:3). As the son of David he is the messianic king expected by Israel. All that has happened in the history of Israel, then, has been in preparation for his coming. Four women are included in the genealogy and in each case there is something unusual about the woman. By this Matthew seems to be drawing attention to the strange ways in which divine providence works and so preparing us for the virgin birth (1:18-25).

Reflection

Family trees are not very interesting until you know

something about the people who are the branches, especially the unsavory characters. Three of the four women named by Matthew in the family tree of Jesus are not exactly the kind of people most of us would be proud to claim as our ancestors.

Tamar deceived her father-in-law, Judah, into an incestuous union. Rahab was a prostitute. And Solomon's mother, Bathsheba, was David's partner in an act of adultery which was followed by the murder of her husband, Uriah. These skeletons could easily have been kept hidden in the family closet, but Matthew chose to open the door for us to peek in. Precisely why he did so is not at all clear. The purpose of the entire genealogy is to show that Jesus Christ is the summit of the salvation history which began with the promise made to Abraham. Perhaps Matthew had in mind the fact that the Savior would be known as a friend of publicans and sinners (Mt. 11:19), that he himself would declare that he had been sent to the lost sheep of the house of Israel (Mt. 15:24), and that even in his death on the cross he would be flanked by two robbers (Mt. 27:38).

Jesus was born to save sinners, not just those named in his genealogy, but all of us. Through the disobedience of "Adam" we were all constituted sinners, but through the loving obedience of Jesus on the cross we were freed from sin. The family tree of the human race, which began with the sinner, Adam, was transformed by the tree on Calvary. How fortunate we are that we can now trace our spiritual genealogy back to Christ, the new head of our human race.

DECEMBER 18

JEREMIAH 23:5-8
In chapter 22 Jeremiah soundly condemns the kings

of Judah. It is they who are responsible for the evils that have befallen the land for by their unjust rule they have misled the people and so brought about their dispersion over the earth. But in the future things will be different says the prophet, speaking in the name of the Lord. For the Lord will raise up a descendant of David who will rule and govern wisely doing what is just and right in the land. This king will receive the name "The Lord our justice," a name which signifies that God is present in him and acting through him to save his people (5-6). At that time the Lord will also bring back to the promised land those who have been scattered into exile and this new act of deliverance will be seen as so wondrous that it will overshadow the exodus of old.

Reflection

On the night before he died, with his apostles gathered around him at the supper table, Jesus prayed to his Father for the unity of his followers: "That they all may be one as we are one" (Jn. 17:21). Jesus wanted us to live together in harmony and peace. That he prayed for this intention on the very night before his death shows how close it was to his heart.

In the Mass, as we gather around the eucharistic supper table to commemorate the death of Jesus, we pray for the same intention: "May all of us who share in the body and blood of Christ be brought together in unity by the Holy Spirit." We offer a sign of peace to those present as an expression of our desire to make this prayer bear fruit in the way in which we live with one another. If we are not living together harmoniously, whom do we have to blame?

Before the time of Christ, the prophet Jeremiah accused the kings of Judah of not guiding the people properly and of therefore being responsible for their dispersion from the promised land. If Jeremiah were alive today he would not blame earthly rulers for any lack of harmony among us. Instead he would stand before us and say, "Don't you realize that you now have a king, a righteous shoot to David, who reigns and governs wisely, who does what is just and right in the land?" He would remind us that we have Jesus Christ, the Messiah-King, present among us not only to guide us in our lives, but also to give us the means of achieving real unity through the Eucharist. He would preach the same doctrine as did St. Paul: "Because the bread is one, we though many, are one body, all of us who partake of the one bread" (1 Cor. 10:17). If we are not living together harmoniously, we really have no one to blame but ourselves, for we have the means of doing so in the Eucharist.

MATTHEW 1:18-25

> *The purpose of this passage is to show how Jesus, who had no human father, was incorporated into the house of David. Namely, it was by Joseph's taking Mary into his house as his wife and his naming of the child, an act of adoption, out of obedience to the divine command. Secondly, the passage points out who Jesus is: he is the promised Savior, but a Savior who will save God's people from their sins not from their human enemies as many of the Jews expected; he is also the one whom Isaiah (7:14) had called "Immanuel," the one through whom God would be in the midst of his people in a very special way. Thirdly, it is being brought out that all that has happened is according to the Scriptures and so part of God's plan for the salvation of man.*

Reflection

Today's gospel shows how Joseph, a descendant of David, took Mary as his wife and adopted her child as his own. The result of his action was that Jesus was incorporated into the house of David in fulfillment of Old

Testament prophecies. But the gospel contains a puzzling element. The angel assured Joseph that he should not fear to take Mary as his wife. What was Joseph afraid of? Knowing Mary, could he possibly have thought that she had been unfaithful to him? If so his reaction would not have been fear, but revulsion and indignation. Moreover, the evangelist clearly states that Mary "was found with child through the power of the Holy Spirit." The person who found her with child through the power of the Holy Spirit could have been only Joseph himself. It was the most natural thing in the world for Mary to confide in him.

Joseph's fear, then, was not about Mary. It was about himself. Humble as he was, he could not see how he of all people should presume to become the husband of someone who had been touched by God. He felt unworthy to take part in so holy a situation. The word of the angel did not give Joseph information but direction—to go ahead with his marriage.

Christmas is appealing to us because it makes God so close to us. Jesus is indeed "Immanuel," God with us in a simple, human way. But we should never allow the simplicity and humanness of Christmas to dull our sense of wonder and awe. We would do well to imitate Joseph in his humility because we are really much less worthy than he, a great saint, to take part in so holy a reality. Humility does not mean backing off in fear from the mystery of Christmas; rather it should move us to praise God for his goodness in calling us to be so close to him in the person of his Son made flesh. As we prepare to celebrate the birth of Jesus Christ our hearts should be filled with wonder and praise.

DECEMBER 19

JUDGES 13:2-7, 24-25
> *Throughout the book of Judges there is a certain pattern. When Israel offended the Lord He delivered her into the hands of her enemies but when Israel called out to the Lord He raised up for her a savior who would deliver her from her enemies. When Israel offended the Lord and was delivered into the power of the Philistines the savior whom the Lord sent was Samson. As other Old Testament heroes Samson is God's gift to a barren woman. The purpose of such wondrous births is to bring out that salvation comes from God. As the one who is to begin the deliverance of Israel from the Philistines he is to be consecrated to the Lord from the womb, i.e., he is to be under the nazirite vow (see Numbers 4). He will accomplish his mission because the spirit of the Lord, God's power, will be with him.*

Reflection

We look upon jealousy, the intolerance of any rival, as being a vice, a flaw of character. And so to speak of God as being jealous strikes us as unthinkable. Yet God is jealous, and in him jealousy is a virtue. It would be both unjust and untruthful for God to allow some rival to receive credit for what he alone accomplishes. And God must be both just and truthful.

In today's lesson we have an example of God's jealousy —perhaps we should say his justice and truthfulness. The people needed a leader like Samson to deliver them from the Philistines. They needed a savior. Samson's being born of a woman who was naturally barren was a sign that God was at work. He was the real savior of his people. We see much the same sign in the gospel narrative of the conception of John the Baptist in the womb of Elizabeth who had been sterile and was advanced in years. This sign of God at work reaches its finest expression in Mary who, though young, conceived Jesus without the cooperation of any human male.

Pelagius, a British monk who lived at the turn of the fifth century, ignored the jealousy of God. He taught that human beings can accomplish good without God's grace. Among us today we have a smattering of Pelagianism in those who see the Eucharist only as an expression of a good life. They insist that it is hypocritical to celebrate the Mass until one has proven his goodness. The Eucharist, it is true, should be an expression of goodness, but it is also a means to goodness. To think that we should not celebrate the Mass until we have arrived at perfection or even near-perfection is to fall into a modern form of Pelagianism. A more subtle form of Pelagianism is found in those who say that it is more important to love your neighbor than it is to bother with the liturgy. That is putting the cart before the horse, the effect before the cause.

The Vatican Council clearly taught that the Eucharist is not only the summit toward which all the activity of the Church is directed but also the font from which all her power flows (*Constitution on the Liturgy*, 10). Jesus rightly said at the last supper, when he instituted the Eucharist, "Apart from me you can do nothing" (Jn. 15:5).

LUKE 1:5-25

Malachi 3:23f had promised that before the Lord Himself came to judge and to save mankind He would send Elijah to prepare the people for his coming. This passage announces that John the Baptist is the fulfillment of that prophecy. Hence, he will not only be a source of joy to his parents as the answer to their prayers but he will also be a source of joy to many others. As one dedicated to God and filled with His salvific power John will move many to repentance and so prepare a well-disposed people for the coming of the Lord. The miraculous birth of this child from old and childless parents brings out that salvation is a gift of God. Zechariah's doubt concerning the word of the Lord results in muteness.

Reflection

Poor Zechariah! In the moment when two life-long desires were fulfilled, he faltered. His first desire had been to have a child. Then when he and his wife were both advanced in years, God told him through the angel that Elizabeth would bear a son. But Zachary doubted. As a devout Jew and a priest he believed without qualification in God's power. He did not doubt that God *could* give him a son in his advanced age; he doubted only that God *would* give him a son. In other words, though he believed in God's power, he did not trust that God loved him enough to use that power in his behalf.

And what a time he chose to falter! For Zechariah's second life-long desire had been to have the privilege of offering incense in the sanctuary of the Lord. Only once in his lifetime did each priest offer incense; having once done so, he was never again given the privilege. It was a privilege determined by the drawing of lots, and through his many years the lot had not fallen on Zechariah. Now in this supreme moment, when God had granted him this priestly favor, at a time above all times when he should have trusted in God's love for him, Zechariah doubted.

We should not judge Zechariah harshly, for God did not reject him in his moment of hesitation. Instead, we should see whether we are not somewhat like Zechariah. We believe in God and everything about him which our faith teaches. But do we really trust that God loves us enough to use his almighty power in our behalf? We do not doubt that God *can* do something for us, but maybe we are not sufficiently convinced that he *will* do it, especially if we have waited a long time. In the supreme moment of the Mass, when God shows us both his power and love, at this time above all times we should trust completely in God, even if we have to wait a lifetime, as did Zechariah, to see God use his almighty power out of love for us.

DECEMBER 20

ISAIAH 7:10-14

The kings of Aram and Israel want Ahaz, king of Judah, to join in an alliance against Assyria. But Ahaz refuses and when he hears that these kings are marching on Jerusalem to overthrow him he decides to ask Assyria for help. Isaiah then comes to Ahaz and tells him: put your faith in the Lord, not in an alliance with Assyria, for in a short time both Israel and Aram will be destroyed while Judah shall remain (7:1-9). Isaiah tells Ahaz to ask for a sign from God, any sign he wishes, that what he has just said will be so. But Ahaz brushes Isaiah aside with a pious platitude and an angry Isaiah tells him a sign will be given to him anyway: a young woman of marriageable age (probably one of the king's wives) will bear a son and name him Immanuel (God with us). The point of the sign seems to be that despite Ahaz' lack of faith Aram and Israel will fail and the Davidic line will continue—a sign that God is truly with His people.

Reflection

Ahaz, king of Judah, was playing a dangerous game with Isaiah the prophet. Ahaz wanted to enter into an alliance with Assyria to protect himself from his neighboring kings. When Isaiah heard of the plan, he insisted that Ahaz should put his trust in God, not in some foreign military power, and even promised him a sign of God's fidelity. Ahaz refused the offer, saying in effect, "I wouldn't be so bold as to ask God for a sign." Actually Ahaz was afraid that if he were to receive a sign he would have to abandon his alliance with Assyria, and the truth was that he had more confidence in the power of Assyria than he did in the power of God.

Isaiah, refusing to play games, gave Ahaz the sign anyway: "The virgin shall be with child and bear a son." This child, a pledge that the kingdom of Judah would survive through a descendant of David, was a sign of God's continued presence and protection. The prophecy of Isaiah, as read in the Church and understood in the light of further revelation, is seen as being eminently fulfilled in the Virgin Mary's son who is truly Immanuel, "God with us" (*Constitution on the Church*, 55).

Through all the difficulty, frustration, and dangers of life, we must learn to depend on God as Ahaz did not. The birth of Jesus Christ from the Virgin Mary stands as a perpetual sign to us of God's continued presence and protection. Soon we will celebrate Christmas, a feast rich in meaning. Today, however, let us reflect on one aspect of that feast: the sign that in Jesus Christ, our Immanuel, God is indeed still with us.

LUKE 1:26-38

The evangelist emphasizes who Jesus is by making the announcement of his birth parallel the announcement of the birth of John (1:5-25). *The reason for the greatness of Jesus* (v. 32) *is that he will be the hoped for Davidic Messiah in whom God will be present redeeming man, and so the fulfillment of all the Old Testament hopes. He truly lives up to his name, Jesus, "Yahweh is salvation." But Jesus will be more than just the Messiah. Since he will be conceived by the power of the Most High of a virgin, he will be in a*

> *real sense, unlike any other man, the Son of God, God present in the world. Secondarily, this passage points to the special place which Mary holds because of God's choice of her to be the mother of the Messiah. Unlike Zechariah Mary does not doubt the word of the Lord but humbly submits to his will.*

Reflection

Two statements of Mary at the time of the annunciation are important for understanding our relationship to God as our Savior: "Let it be done to me" and "I am the maidservant of the Lord."

First, "Let it be done to me." Sin came into the world through human free will, and God wanted salvation to come into the world equally through human free will. And so the angel was sent to Mary to seek her consent to the Incarnation. St. Thomas Aquinas taught that Mary, like a new Eve, the mother of all the living, gave her consent in the name of the whole human race (III, q. 30, a. 1), an opinion supported by Pope Pius XII in his encyclical on the Mystical Body (127). When Mary said, "Let it be done to me," the salvation of the world through Jesus Christ began (cf. also the *Constitution on the Church*, 55-56). Though Mary consented to salvation in our name, we must confirm that consent, each one for himself. God wills the salvation of all men, but he respects human freedom so much that he forces his salvation on no one. God will not give us salvation without our cooperation.

But it is not quite that simple. We must remember the second statement of Mary, "I am the maidservant of the Lord." A maidservant is one who is totally dependent on her master, and Mary in her humility, her honesty, recognized that she was totally dependent on God. As such, not even Mary could have given her consent without God's grace. And we are so totally dependent on God that we cannot freely consent to our salvation unless he moves us to do so. Though it is beyond our comprehension, God has the power to move us to accept salvation without destroying our freedom.

Complicated? Yes, but it is vital to recognize that while we must work for our salvation, salvation is still a gift since the work itself cannot be done without God. Salvation is so gratuitous that without God we cannot even say "yes" to the salvation he freely offers us. Like Mary we should say, "Let it be done to me," but all the while we must realize that, like Mary, we are totally dependent on God.

DECEMBER 21

SONG OF SONGS 2:8-14

This is part of one of the many love songs that make up the Song of Songs. In this song the girl speaks describing the approach of her lover bounding over the hills like a young stag toward her house. Once there he invites her to come outside with him to walk in the fields for it is springtime and the flowers are blooming, the birds singing and the vines are giving forth their fragrance. The song concludes with the young man once again inviting her out to join him. Traditionally, these love songs have been interpreted as describing symbolically the love between God and Israel. The girl would be Israel, the lover, God, and the springtime would refer to God's expected renewal of Israel when He comes.

Reflection

The love song in the first lesson today is one of many in the Bible which have traditionally been understood as symbolic of the love between God and his people. These songs celebrate young love: a thrilling, absorbing, ardent affection, an attachment which is tender, yet strong, unselfish, yet fulfilling.

Young love is a wonderful symbol of God's love for us, but there is one big difference. Young love in time tends to weaken with familiarity; its luster grows dim with routine; its ardor lessens in the harshness of daily living. Not so with God's love. His love is constant, unchanging, and always faithful.

Young love is also a symbol of our love for God. Perhaps we have never quite felt the intensity of young love in our relationship with God, but it is very likely that our feeling of love has weakened with familiarity, its luster has grown dim with routine, its ardor has lessened in the harshness of life.

It is often said that love is blind, but that is not true. Real love sees attributes in another which no one else has the vision to perceive. And yet familiarity, like a cataract, obscures the vision of love. Our familiarity with even the signs of God's love can dull our vision. One of these familiar signs is the mystery of Christmas: God so loved the world that in the fullness of time he sent his only son to be our savior. But the feast of Christmas contains a light bright enough to get through our dimmed vision if we look intently enough with faith at this great mystery. We should pray that this year we may see the birth of Jesus Christ in such a light that our love for God may become more like his love for us.

ZEPHANIAH 3:14-18

> *This is an invitation to the city of Jerusalem to be joyful for her salvation is at hand. She is to rejoice because on the day of salvation the Lord Himself will be in her midst removing from her the punishment for her sins and destroying her enemies. So she is to put aside her fear because the Lord as a mighty savior will be in her midst, rejoicing over her and renewing her out of his love for her.*

Reflection

Christmas carols help to heighten our feelings at this time of the year. A very popular carol begins, "Joy to the world, the Savior reigns; let earth receive her king." If there is one emotion which should be ours at Christmas, it is joy.

The prophet Zephaniah proclaimed joy to the faithful of Judah even during a time of religious degradation when in the city of Jerusalem itself some had fallen into idolatrous worship of the sun, the moon, and the stars. His proclamation looked to the future, to a great day of the Lord when once again it would be said to Jerusalem, "The Lord, your God, is in your midst, a mighty savior."

We too live in an era of idolatry when some worship materialism and pleasure. God proclaims joy to us in our celebration of Christmas as we look to the past to see the coming of the Lord, a mighty savior, into our world. Our Christmas joy, however, is not derived only from the past. It is also a present reality and a future hope. The birth of Jesus is more than history. In a real sense by the power of God Jesus is born in each of us through our Christmas liturgy. His coming is as fresh and new for us as it was for Mary his mother. The liturgy proclaims "The Lord, your God, is in your midst, a mighty savior." And like Zephaniah we also look to the future, for though Christ is present he is also yet to come on the great day of the Lord. And what a festival of joy that day will be when the whole world receives her king!

As Christians, as the faithful of the Lord, we should sing in our hearts: "Joy to the world, the Savior reigns; let earth receive her king."

Luke 1:39-45
> *The contrast between John and Jesus is now made explicit. The child in the womb of Elizabeth leaps at*

the presence of Mary pregnant with Jesus. By this Luke wishes to stress once again the superiority of Jesus over John and John's recognition of that fact. Elizabeth, enlightened by the Spirit, recognizes the significance of the movement in her womb and praises Mary as more blessed than all women because she is the mother of the Lord. Elizabeth also praises Mary for her trust in the word of the Lord.

Reflection

For a very long time Elizabeth and her husband, Zechariah, had prayed and yearned for a child as a fruit of their marriage. When Elizabeth finally conceived in her old age, when all natural hope for a child had been exhausted, she recognized that she had been specially blessed by God. She was awed by the miracle which had taken place in her womb. But when Elizabeth saw her cousin, and the child stirred in her womb, she realized that an even greater work of God was present in Mary. Enlightened by the Holy Spirit she cried out to Mary: "Blessed are you among women and blessed is the fruit of your womb." She was so awed by the miracle which had taken place in Mary's womb that she felt unworthy even to be in her presence: "Who am I that the mother of my Lord should come to me?"

We have received many blessings from God, none perhaps as dramatic as that granted to Elizabeth and Zechariah, but striking nonetheless. We should praise and thank God for all these favors, but at this time of the year we must think especially about the meaning of Christmas: God himself comes to us in the person of his son made flesh in the womb of Mary. We need to reflect on this great mystery of God's love for us. Each one of us, in awe and wonder, should ask, "Who am I that the Lord himself should come to me?" Before receiving Jesus in holy communion we are invited to confess, "Lord, I am not worthy to receive you." We are not worthy indeed, and if we had only a natural hope of receiving God's favor we would have to turn away from the table of the Lord in despair. But the Holy Spirit enlightens us to see that, though we are not worthy, God loves us so much that he wishes to give us the great gift of his own son. And that is really something to praise and thank God for.

DECEMBER 22

1 SAMUEL 1:24-28

Samuel, as Samson, was God's gift to a barren woman (see FIRST READING *for* DECEMBER 19*). Hannah, Samuel's mother, had prayed to the Lord asking for a son and had promised the Lord that if He would grant her wish she would offer her son to the Lord as a perpetual nazirite, i.e., as one consecrated to the service of the Lord (see 1 S. 1:11-22). Hence, when Samuel was weaned (probably around age three), she brought him along with an offering to the Temple of the Lord at Shilo to fulfill her vow. There she handed him over to the priest, Eli, who had witnessed her prayer to the Lord for a son (1 S. 1-9f).*

Reflection

Hannah had prayed long and earnestly for a son and promised that if her prayer were answered she would consecrate her child to the Lord. Today's lesson recounts how after Samuel was born to her, she and her husband presented the child to the Lord together with the sacrifice of a young bull. Samuel became their gift to God, and they left him in the temple.

One of the most difficult things for devoted parents to do is to let go of their children. Even if parents do not desire a child as earnestly as did Hannah, when he does come along they usually become very attached to him. Every child, whether eagerly or reluctantly accepted, is given to parents only for a while. Ties must eventually be broken so that a child may have the freedom to fulfill his own purpose in life. Children do not belong completely to their parents.

Perhaps parental ties could be severed with less pain if each one of us were to realize that we do not belong completely even to ourselves. We belong to God. He is the one parent with whom ties should never be broken. True freedom means giving ourselves totally to him, for that is the purpose of life. We must do for ourselves what Hannah did for Samuel as she offered him to the Lord.

In the third Eucharistic Prayer, wherein we offer to God the sacrifice of his own Son, we say these words: "May he make us an everlasting gift to you." An everlasting gift—that means an offering which is never taken back and a giving which has no reservations. The only way to real happiness in this life and in the next is to put ourselves with trust and love in the hands of God so that he may do with us as he wills.

LUKE 1:46-56

In this song of thanksgiving Mary gives all the honor and glory for what has happened to her to God. Out of His mercy He has done great things for her because of her faith and dependence upon Him. As a result of these things that God has worked in her all ages will praise her (46-50). But the way that God has acted with her is not surprising but quite consistent with the way He has always used His might: raising the lowly to high places and giving the hungry all good things (51-53). But it is not because of what He has done for her that Mary thanks the Lord, but also for fulfilling, through His actions in her, all the promises He had made to Israel from Abraham on (54-55).

Reflection

Christmas in our society is supremely a day for children. What a joyful, happy time it is for them as they open their presents and begin to play with their toys! Adults too want to share their simple pleasures. We have developed almost a caricature of that attitude in the picture of a father who spends more time in playing with an electric train than does his son to whom the present was given.

Actually Christmas is not meant for children any more than it is for adults. It is meant for anyone, whatever his age, who has faith and humility as Mary did. When Elizabeth praised her for being given the gift of Jesus Christ as her son, Mary manifested how profound was her faith and how great was her humility: "My spirit finds joy in God my savior, for he has looked upon his servant in her lowliness."

To feel the joy of Christmas we must have the faith to believe that the almighty God himself came into our world in the flesh of an infant. To experience the thrill of Christmas, we must accept the awesome paradox that, as G. K. Chesterton expressed it, in the cave of Bethlehem "the hands that had made the sun and the stars were too small to reach the huge heads of the cattle." To derive benefit from Christmas, we have to receive Jesus Christ as God's special gift to us, to open our arms to embrace him, to let him become a part of our lives, as Mary did. And even if we are mature adults, with serious responsibilities, we must be humble enough to admit that we need Jesus, that without him we cannot make any sense of our lives or accomplish any worthwhile purpose.

All the happiness which should be a part of Christmas can be ours if we join Mary in saying, "My spirit finds joy in God my savior, for he has looked upon his servant in her lowliness."

DECEMBER 23

MALACHI 3:1-4, 23-24

After the exile the Jews who returned to the promised land had to struggle to survive and they began to accuse God of not being just because it seemed like only the evildoers prospered. The people wanted to know when this just God would intervene and fulfill His promises of blessings to the just. Here Malachi tells the people that the coming of the Lord is close at hand. First He will send a messenger to prepare the way but then the Lord Himself will come, like a refiner's fire. He will first come to the Temple and there purify the priests of their sins so that they can once again offer worthy and pleasing sacrifices to Him (1-4). Verses 23-24 are a later addition whose purpose is to identify the messenger of 3:1. The messenger is said to be Elijah who will return to earth (see 2 K. 2:11) to try to reconcile mankind lest total doom strike the land.

Reflection

Today's lesson does not seem to be in accord with the joyful spirit of Christmas. Malachi told the people that the Lord would come, which sounds cheerful enough, but he warned them that the Lord would purify them as silver and gold are refined in fire, which sounds somewhat ominous.

An old proverb is applicable here: one man's meat is another man's poison. The point of Malachi's prophecy was that the coming of the Lord would be painful only for those who were not ready, and he said that Elijah, the prophet, would come first to prepare the people. Jesus himself stated that this Elijah, this special prophet, was actually John the Baptist (cf. Mt. 11:10ff).

John came preaching repentance as a preparation for the Messiah. Repentance means a turning away from sin and a turning toward God. Part of our Christmas preparation has traditionally been the making of a good confession and that is a practice in accord with the message of the Baptist, as we make use of this sacrament in order to turn away from sin. From this sacrament we should also seek to derive the grace to turn our thoughts to God, to center upon Christmas as a spiritual celebration of God's love for us in the coming of his Son. Many good people lament the commercialism which has obscured this spiritual meaning of Christmas, but it seems better to make a positive use of today's Christmas practices. The giving of gifts should make us think of God's Christmas gift to us. Christmas carols, even nonsensical ones like *Jingle Bells*, help to create an atmosphere of joy, an emotion which should be ours at this time. A big Christmas dinner can remind us that God calls us to share in the spiritual banquet of the Mass, which is a foreshadowing of our eternal blessedness in heaven.

The so-called material aspects of Christmas don't have to be our poison. They can be a refreshing nourishment which helps us open our eyes with renewed vigor to the true beauties of our Christmas celebration.

LUKE 1:57-66
> *In this passage we find the fulfillment of the Lord's word that Elizabeth would bear a son as also a partial fulfillment of the promise that many would rejoice at John's birth (v. 14). Circumcision, which took place on the eighth day after the birth of a male child, was a very important event for it was a male child's initiation into the covenanted people of God. It had become customary at this time to also name the child on this day. Elizabeth and Zechariah, to the surprise of all and against the custom of time, insist on naming the child John according to the word of the Lord (v. 13). With this the spirit of prophecy comes upon Zechariah (see v. 41f) and he praises God (vv. 67-79). The reaction of the people is fear and wonder con-*

cerning this child upon whom the hand of the Lord appeared to rest.

Reflection

William Shakespeare in *Romeo and Juliet* wrote, "What's in a name? That which we call a rose by any other name would smell as sweet." People's names don't have much significance these days, and yet, though we don't often reflect on it, some surnames, such as Farmer or Baker, apparently evolved from a person's occupation. Biblical names are often rich in meaning. God himself insisted that the son of Zechariah and Elizabeth be named John for a very good reason. That name in Hebrew literally means "The Lord has shown favor." The Baptist was the last of the Old Testament prophets, and in a sense he summed up in his person all the favors God had shown to the chosen people through his spokesmen, the prophets. Everything that God did in the Old Testament pointed to the person for whom John was to be the herald, Jesus Christ.

John's extraordinary conception and birth as the herald of Christ were the last steps in God's preparation for the saving mission of the Messiah. Nor were his parents' names a matter of chance. "Elizabeth" means "The Lord has sworn," and recalls the solemn promise God made to send the Messiah. "Zechariah" means "The Lord has remembered," and indicates the faithfulness of God in keeping those promises.

What's in a name? In the names of the three principal characters of today's gospel we have a symbol of what our celebration of Christmas ought to be. Our hearts should be filled with praise and thanks to God for having remembered his promises, and for having made us the recipients of his great favor through the person of his Son, born into our world to be our savior.

DECEMBER 24

2 SAMUEL 7:1-5, 8-11, 16
> *Once David has captured Jerusalem and brought the ark there, he thinks about building a temple, a house for the ark, the symbol of God's presence among His people. Nathan, the prophet, at first goes along with the idea but then he receives a message for David from the Lord. The Lord tells David that he is not to build a house for Him but rather that He, God, will establish a house for David that will endure forever, i.e., God promises David an everlasting dynasty. Moreover, God tells David that just as it was He who had chosen David to be king and given him success, so He will now make David famous and through him give Israel peace (rest) from all her enemies. With this last point the text is pointing out that with David God is fulfilling the promises He made to the patriarchs to give Israel "rest" in a land of their own.*

Reflection

David told Nathan the prophet that he wanted to build a house for the Lord, meaning a beautiful temple. God in his turn, through a play on words, told David that he would establish a house for him, meaning a royal dynasty, which we have come to refer to as the "house of David." This promise of God, spoken through Nathan, became the basis of Jewish expectation of a kingly messiah, son of David—an expectation which Jesus Christ, born of the house of David in David's city of Bethlehem, fulfilled in an eminent way.

God's promise contained the idea that people were more important than a temple, that God would work out his plan of salvation through human beings who would prepare for the coming of Christ. When Jesus Christ did come, God's preference for people did not change. People are more important than the physical structure of a church, however appropriate and beautiful. As God chose people to lead up to the coming of Christ, so now he chooses people to continue the presence of his son in the world. We are those people, a chosen race, a royal priesthood.

Through faith and God's grace Jesus Christ is present within us, but his presence can grow. Or perhaps it is better to say that we can grow in our openness to accept him. The ocean is there. Only the container we bring limits how much of it we can take. In our liturgical celebration of Christmas Jesus wants to be born anew in us. He invites us to open our hearts to receive him. Are you willing to let Jesus take over your being, to flood your mind and body with his presence so that through you he may spread his kingdom on earth? His kingdom is one of justice, love, and peace. It is worth the effort to have a share in bringing that kingdom to all men.

LUKE 1:67-79

> *In the first part of this messianic hymn God is praised for having intervened in history to bring salvation and redemption to His people through the Messiah as He had promised by the prophets (68-71). This merciful action of God is the fulfillment of the covenant He had made with Abraham that He would one day deliver His people from their enemies so that they could constantly serve Him unmolested (72-75). In the second part of the hymn John is presented as the prophet foretold by Malachi (3:23f) who would go before the Lord (Jesus) to prepare the way for him by making the people aware that true salvation consists in the forgiveness of sins (76-77). The Hymn concludes by pointing out that all this is due to the faithful love of God. The messianic age is now present and the darkness of sin will be dissipated so that men can faithfully serve God (78-79).*

Reflection

Zechariah thought that in his old body and that of his wife, Elizabeth, there was no hope for a child, for the gift of life. He hesitated to believe that God loved him enough to use his almighty power in his favor. As such Zechariah is a symbol of modern man with all his doubts and anxieties. It is not surprising that in the face of war and hatred, greed and injustice, people are pushed to the edge of despair. The young accuse the old of having made a mess of the world, and the old blame the young for only making it worse. Our world in the view of some is too decrepit to contain any hope for a new life.

Zechariah changed his view when he received a sign from God. That sign was the birth of his son, John. In response to this evident work of God, the old man sang the beautiful song found in today's gospel. In it he praised the faithful love of God.

If at times we are tempted to share in a pessimistic world view, we should remember that we too have received a sign from God. That sign is the birth of God's own son, Jesus Christ. And it is a sign which is not confined to the past, for it becomes a present reality in our liturgical celebration of Christmas. Every Christmas is a testimony from God that he has not given up on the world. Zechariah's song should become our Christmas hymn: "Blessed be the Lord the God of Israel because he has visited and ransomed his people. He has raised a horn of saving strength for us in the house of David his servant."

PART THREE

Saints' Days During Advent

November 30
FEAST OF ST. ANDREW, APOSTLE

ROMANS 10:9-18
> *In chapters nine and ten Paul answers the question of where the blame is to be placed for Israel's not accepting Christ. It is not God who is to be blamed, but Israel. Israel was so zealous in seeking salvation through fulfillment of the law that she neither recognized the Messiah when he came nor God's new way of salvation, the way of faith (10:1-4). The new way of salvation is open to all men through the mercy of God, and is really much easier than the arduous task of an exact keeping of the law. All that is demanded is an interior assent that the Risen Christ is the Lord and an outward confession of this faith (5-13). In verses 14-18 Paul points out that Israel's lack of faith was her own fault; accredited preachers have presented the good news to her (14-15), and the fact that she has not accepted the gospel does not mean that it was not preached to her (16-17). All have had the opportunity to hear the gospel (18).*

MATTHEW 4, 18-22
> *Jesus here calls his first disciples. Two distinct calls take place but the same pattern is followed in each: Jesus sees some fishermen at work whom he calls to follow him and these men immediately drop what they are doing to follow him. The emphasis in the episodes is on the immediacy and unconditioned character of the response of these men to the call. We are not even told whether they knew Jesus before this! Though the first pair of brothers abandon only their nets, the second pair abandon boat and father. In following Jesus one must leave all else behind. A hint of what these men are being called for (the apostolic office) is given when Jesus tells them that he will make them "fishers of men."*

Reflection

The feast of St. Andrew seems to be out of harmony with the season of Advent just when we are beginning to prepare to celebrate the birth of Jesus Christ. As a matter of fact, St. Andrew the Apostle helps to put the Christmas mystery into proper perspective. St. Andrew lived in the shadow of his more famous brother, St. Peter, so that we do not know a whole lot about him. Several very ancient traditions, however, assert that Andrew, like Jesus himself, met death by means of crucifixion. From the day that Andrew accepted, without any conditions, the invitation of Jesus, "Come after me," he was headed for the cross.

It is understandable that we would like to share in the resurrection of Christ without the cross, to gain life without death, to enjoy happiness without suffering. But today's feast reminds us that when Jesus took human flesh, he made himself vulnerable. When he was born into our world, he opened himself to the necessity of suffering physically, mentally, and emotionally. According to the plan of the Father as revealed in Jesus Christ, resurrection comes through the cross, life through death, and happiness through suffering.

When we accepted the invitation, "Come after me," as did Andrew, we made ourselves vulnerable. We opened ourselves to the necessity of suffering with Christ physically, mentally, and emotionally. Advent preparation for Christmas should indeed be joyful, but our joy should be put into proper perspective. According to the plan of the Father, if we wish to share in the lasting happiness of Jesus, we must also be willing to share in his cross as well.

December 3
MEMORIAL OF ST. FRANCIS XAVIER

READINGS FROM THE CURRENT WEEKDAY OF ADVENT

Reflection

What an extraordinary man was St. Francis Xavier! As a missionary he preached the gospel of Jesus Christ in Japan and six other countries of the Far East. His name, "Xavier," in Spanish means "Savior," and true to his name he brought Jesus the Savior to a vast number of people. His converts numbered in the hundreds of thousands. Exhausted by his labors, he died in 1552 in Sancian, an island off the coast of China, far from his home in Spain.

This great saint was mindful of the fact that Jesus came to save all men, no matter who they were or where they happened to live. Quite appropriately Pope Pius X made him patron of the missions. Even though we are not missionaries to some distant country, we can and should follow the example of St. Francis in our own way. At Christmas time we recall that Jesus was born into our world as the savior. We should be grateful that through our faith as Catholics we have accepted the meaning of his coming. But there is more. The name, "Catholic," means "universal." To be a true Catholic we must have a universal interest in our fellow human beings. We are surrounded by a vast number of people for whom the faith of Jesus Christ has little or no meaning, people who are in as much need as were the people of the Orient in the sixteenth century. Why are we so timid and so reluctant to speak of Christ to others? Why are we so unwilling to make even a little effort when a man like St. Francis made a supreme sacrifice to spread the truth of our religion? Today we should pray that God may give us a share in the great zeal and courage of St. Francis Xavier.

By bringing the truth of Jesus Christ to others we can be true to our name, the name of "Catholic."

December 7
MEMORIAL OF ST. AMBROSE, BISHOP

READINGS FROM THE CURRENT WEEKDAY OF ADVENT

Reflection

The memory of St. Ambrose is kept on December 7th because it was on this day in the year 374 that he became a bishop. This saint, in keeping with his office as teacher of the Church in the diocese of Milan, wrote extensively on the role and importance of Mary in our salvation (in his treatise on virginity). His emphasis should remind us that there is no Christmas without Mary, no crib without the Virgin, no Christ Child without his mother.

Celebrating Christmas without Mary is worse than celebrating the Fourth of July without the flag. The flag is only a symbol of our country, but Mary as mother is the true sign that God actually did become human like us in all things but sin. Mary is our link with divinity. Within her womb the divine Son of God took human flesh. In the temple of her body a unique wedding took place, the joining of divinity and humanity in the person of Jesus Christ. From her the God-Man was born into this world of ours in order to accomplish the work of our salvation.

Christmas is a day surrounded with tenderness and emotion, but it is not by mere sentiment that we include Mary in our celebration. She is an integral part of the mystery of Christ's coming.

I think St. Ambrose is pleased by our taking his memorial as an occasion to emphasize once again the place of Mary in the great truth of the birth of Jesus Christ.

December 8
SOLEMNITY OF THE IMMACULATE CONCEPTION

GENESIS 3:9-15, 20
> The first eleven chapters of Genesis explain why God has chosen only one nation out of all the nations as his special people, namely, to bring salvation to the other nations through this one nation (Gn. 12, 1-3). Man needs salvation because he is under a curse from God for his sins. In this passage we have first the dialogue between God and man in the Garden after man's sin of disobedience. Then in verses 14-15 we read the curse of God upon the serpent. This curse is first of all an attempt to explain the serpent's place in nature and the enmity between it and the other animals and man. In so far as the serpent is the symbol of evil in this story the curse foretells the continuing struggle that there will be between man and evil. Implicit in the passage is the promise that ultimately evil will not overcome man but will be destroyed by man since man will strike at the head of the serpent whereas the serpent will strike only at the heel of man. Hence, man can affirm that there will be life (v. 20).

EPHESIANS 1:3-6, 11-12
> Paul begins this letter with a beautiful prayer of thanksgiving (1, 3-14). God, who is the Father of Jesus Christ the Lord, is praised for having freely bestowed upon the Church, i.e., upon those who are united with Christ through their incorporation into a visible community under his rule, "every spiritual blessing in the heavens." These spiritual blessings refer to those blessings which are communicated through Christ, who now rules at the Father's right hand in the heavenly places, to those who are now one with Christ. In the

following verses Paul delineates these blessings: that God on his own initiative has chosen us, has called us to faith, from all eternity in order that we might be holy and blameless through the practice of love (4) *and that we might be his adopted sons in order that we might praise him for all he has done for us* (5-6).

LUKE 1, 26-38

The evangelist emphasizes who Jesus is by making the announcement of his birth parallel the announcement of the birth of John (1:5-25). *The reason for the greatness of Jesus is that he will be the hoped for Davidic Messiah in whom God will be present redeeming man, and so the fulfillment of all the Old Testament hopes. He truly lives up to his name, Jesus, "Yahweh is salvation." But Jesus will be more than just the Messiah for, since he will be conceived by the power of the Most High of a virgin, he will be in a real sense, unlike any other man, the Son of God, God present in the world. Secondly, this passage points to the special place which Mary holds because of God's choice of her to be the mother of the Messiah. Unlike Zechariah Mary does not doubt the word of the Lord but humbly submits to his will.*

Reflection

A mother is a special person. No matter what our human relationships may be through the years, the relationship with our mother remains unique. We began life within the safe, protective confines of her womb. There we were nourished and grew until we were born. And though the cord uniting us to our mother was severed at birth, our union with her was not broken. We were fed at her breast and consoled in her warm embrace. Later we listened for the loving words of her gentle voice, and we told her of our needs and worries, our joy and happiness. Yes, a mother is a very special person. And yet as we grew older we realized that our mother, however wonderful, was not perfect, for she was as human as we.

It is no wonder that Jesus wanted his mother to be perfect. Because he was divine and pre-existed his mother, he could fashion his mother exactly as he pleased. He brought to bear on her his almighty power as he preserved her free of original sin from the time of her conception. It was a unique privilege befitting the unique relationship between Jesus and Mary. The immaculate conception is an Advent feast, for Mary was preserved from sin so that she could be a worthy source from whom the Son of God would be born into the world. She was conceived immaculate in her mother's womb for the moment described in today's gospel when Jesus was conceived in her womb.

Even though we have not shared in the immaculate conception, this privilege of Mary has meaning for us. It is more than a family secret which has been told us as we peer in from the outside. It is more than a humanly appealing fact, that in God's plan a perfect woman is inseparably connected with the coming of the savior. Perhaps above all, Mary's immaculate conception should stand as a sign of hope to us since it reveals the greatest masterpiece of the savior's power. In 1821 William Wordsworth wrote these beautiful verses of Mary:

> *Mother! whose virgin bosom was uncrost*
> *With the least shade of thought to sin allied;*
> *Woman above all women glorified,*
> *Our tainted nature's solitary boast. . . .**

We should boast about Mary. We should cry out to the whole world: "See what the power of Christ has done for a member of our race." And therein lies our hope. If the power of the savior is great enough to preserve Mary, a human person like ourselves, from sin, then it is great

---

*Ecclesiastical Sonnets, Part II, no. 25, "The Virgin."

enough to cure us of the effects of sin.

As we make our Advent preparations we should recognize with humility and honesty that we are not worthy of God. And yet God wants us. St. Paul reminds us of our calling (second reading): "God chose us in Christ before the world began, to be holy and blameless in his sight, to be full of love. . . ." As we look at ourselves we should be able to see that we are far from our calling. But that is no reason for discouragement. Remember that the same savior who preserved Mary free from sin wishes to cleanse us from sin.

In the Mass before communion we proclaim: "Lord, I am not worthy to receive you, but only say the word and I shall be healed." What is this word of healing? Its finest expression is found in the sacrament of penance when Jesus says through the priest, "I absolve you from your sins." That word of Jesus both repairs injuries of the past and gives strength for the future. Confession is a traditional part of our preparation for Christmas, and that practice should continue. We are not immaculate as was Mary, but because of her immaculate conception we should have the confidence that through confession we can prepare ourselves to receive the grace of Christ at Christmas. His grace can lead us to our calling, to be holy and blameless and full of love.

December 13
MEMORIAL OF ST. LUCY, MARTYR

READINGS FROM THE CURRENT WEEKDAY OF ADVENT

Reflection

The feast of St. Lucy is a very ancient one, its celebration dating back to the sixth century in Rome. She has been honored in the Church ever since because she went to her death rather than abandon her faith. And yet it is an aspect of her life rather than her death which makes her celebration appropriate for the season of Advent. According to the traditional story told about her, when Lucy came of age she asked her mother for her dowry. Instead of using the money, according to the custom of the day, to secure a husband, she gave all her money to the poor. Her generosity to God's poor was greater than her natural desire for marriage and a family of her own.

During Advent we are thinking about the gifts we will give at Christmas. Isn't it true that for the most part we give gifts to persons who are very close to us, people who usually respond by giving us a gift in return. There is nothing wrong with that. We should give gifts to people as a sign of our love for them. But think about St. Lucy. She gave her gifts to people who were really in need, people who could not return the favor. Perhaps we could do well on this feast of St. Lucy to reflect on the fact that we should develop a greater spirit of generosity in our Christmas celebration. A good resolution would be to make sure that we help someone who really has a serious need. And if we want to be as generous as possible, we can give the gift anonymously. That way we can be sure that we won't even be looking for a "thank you" in return.

St. Lucy is a good model for our Christmas giving.

December 14
MEMORIAL OF ST. JOHN OF THE CROSS

READINGS FROM THE CURRENT WEEKDAY OF ADVENT

Reflection

St. John of the Cross died at the age of forty-nine after

having lived a laborious and difficult life. He wrote several books on prayer and the spiritual life which are classics and which reflect his own inner struggle to grow in his love for God. Most of his prayer was a reliving of the prayer of Jesus in Gethsemane, "Not my will but yours be done." He expended much effort in reforming the Carmelite Order, of which he was a member, but his good intentions often met with resistance and rebuffs. Like Jesus, "to his own he came, yet his own did not accept him."

It is related that when St. John was coming to the end of his life, Jesus appeared to him and asked what reward he desired. He replied, "Lord, to suffer and to be despised for you." And that, to a large extent, is what makes the difference between St. John of the Cross and ourselves. He had the courage *to ask* to suffer and be despised. I for one do not have that same courage, but I do recognize that like this saint all of us are required to suffer and to be despised.

Advent is a time for becoming more aware of the kind of life Jesus led when he took flesh and became one of us. It is also a time for becoming more like Jesus in our own lives. St. John of the Cross reminds us that becoming like Jesus involves the need to suffer and be despised. Our prayer becomes a form of suffering when we have to battle against distractions and boredom, and struggle to say and mean, "Not my will but yours be done." Our best intentions will at times meet with resistance and rebuffs, even from those whom we love the most. Perseverance will win a reward, not indeed the one St. John asked for, but the one he merited: a life of perfect happiness with Jesus when he comes again in glory.

INDEX TO BIBLICAL PASSAGES

OLD TESTAMENT—DAY

Genesis
3:9-15; 20 — Dec 8
49:2; 8-10 — Dec 17
Numbers
24:2-7; 15-17 — Mon of 3
Judges
13:2-7; 24-25 — Dec 19
1 Samuel
1:24-28 — Dec 22
2 Samuel
7:1-5; 8-11; 16 — Dec 24
Song of Songs
2:8-10 — Dec 21
Sirach
48:1-4; 9-11 — Sat of 2
Isaiah
2:1-5 — Mon of 1
4:2-6 — Mon of 1
7:10-14 — Dec 20
11:1-10 — Tu of 1
25:6-10 — Wed of 1
26:1-6 — Th of 1
29:17-24 — Fr of 1
30:19-21; 23-26 — Sat of 1
35:1-10 — Mon of 2
40:1-11 — Tu of 2
40:25-31 — Wed of 2
41:13-20 — Th of 2
45:6-8; 18; 21-25 — Wed of 3
48:17-19 — Fr of 2
54:1-10 — Th of 3
56:1-3; 6-8 — Fr of 3
Jeremiah
23:5-8 — Dec 18
Zephaniah
3:1-2; 9-13 — Tu of 3
3:14-18 — Dec 21
Malachi
3:1-4; 23-24 — Dec 23

NEW TESTAMENT—DAY

Matthew
1:1-17 — Dec 17
1:18-24 — Dec 18
4:18-22 — Nov 30
7:21; 24-27 — Th of 1
8:5-11 — Mon of 1
9:27-31 — Fr of 1
9:35-10:1; 6-8 — Sat of 1
11:11-15 — Th of 2
11:16-19 — Fr of 2
11:28-30 — Wed of 2
15:29-37 — Wed of 1
17:10-13 — Sat of 2
18:12-14 — Tu of 2
21:23-27 — Mon of 3
21:28-32 — Tu of 3
Luke
1:5-25 — Dec 19
1:26-38 — Dec 8 and 20
1:39-45 — Dec 21
1:46-56 — Dec 22
1:57-66 — Dec 23
1:67-79 — Dec 24
5:17-26 — Mon of 2
7:18-23 — Wed of 3
7:24-30 — Th of 3
10:21-24 — Tu of 1
John
5:33-36 — Fr of 3
Romans
10:9-18 — Nov 30
Ephesians
1:3-6; 11-12 — Dec 8